D1036688

A HISTORY OF
MULTICULTURAL AMERICA

The Great Society to the Reagan Era
1964-1990

William Loren Katz

RSVP

RAINTREE
STECK-VAUGHN
P U B L I S H E R S
The Steck-Vaughn Company

Austin, Texas

Copyright © 1993 Steck-Vaughn Company

Cover and interior design: Joyce Spicer
Electronic production: Scott Melcer
Photo editor: Margie Foster
Photo research: Diane Hamilton

Library of Congress Cataloging-in-Publication Data

Katz, William Loren.
 The Great Society to the Reagan era, 1964-1990 / by William Loren Katz.
  p.   cm. — (A History of multicultural America)
 Includes bibliographical references and index.
 Summary: Discusses the role of minorities and women in American history and society from 1964 to 1990.
  ISBN 0-8114-6282-X   —   ISBN 0-8114-2919-9 (soft cover)
  1. Pluralism (Social sciences) — United States — History — 20th century — Juvenile literature. 2. Minorities — United States — History — 20th century — Juvenile literature. 3. Civil rights movements — United States — History — 20th century — Juvenile literature. 4. United States — History — 1961-1969 — Juvenile literature. 5. United States — History — 1969- — Juvenile literature. 6. United States — Race relations — Juvenile literature. [1. Minorities — History — 20th century. 2. Civil rights movements — History — 20th century. 3. Race relations. 4. United States — History — 1961-1969 5. United States — History — 1969-] I. Title. II. Series: Katz, William Loren. History of multicultural America.
 E184.A1K299   1993
 973.92—dc20   92-43709
                                                              CIP
                                                              AC

Printed and bound in the United States of America

  4 5 6 7 8 9 0 LB 98 97 96 95 94

Acknowledgments

All prints from the collection of the author, William L. Katz, with the following exceptions: pp. 7, 26b, 31, 37, 56, 60, 63t, 63b, 67b, 68, 71, 74, 79 Library of Congress; pp. 9, 13, 14, 50b National Archives; pp. 11, 12, 17, 21, 22, 48, 52, 59, 63c, 64, 65b, 66, 67t, 90 UPI/Bettmann; pp. 18, 54, 65t, 69 AP/Wide World; pp. 19, 27, 58t Life Magazine; p. 23 © Bob Fitch/Black Star; p. 26t © Black Star; p. 28 Defense Department, Marine Corps; pp. 29, 30 U.S. Army; p. 32 United Nations; pp. 33, 34, 35, 41, 43 (both), 49, 72, 75, 84, 88, 91 Washington Star Collection; p. 36 Santa Barbara News-Press; pp. 57, 86 Supreme Court Historical Society.

Cover: (inset) © Martha Cooper/City Lore.; (map) © 1993 by Rand McNally
R.L. 93-S-20

TABLE OF CONTENTS

INTRODUCTION

The history of the United States is the story of people of many backgrounds. A few became wealthy through their knowledge of science, industry, or banking. But it was ordinary people who most shaped the progress of this country and created our national heritage.

The American experience, however, has often been recounted in history books as the saga of powerful men—presidents and senators, merchants and industrialists. Schoolchildren were taught that the wisdom and patriotism of an elite created democracy and prosperity.

A truthful history of the United States has to do more than celebrate the contributions of the few. Ordinary Americans fought the Revolution that set this country free, and ordinary workers built the nation's economy. The overwhelming majority of people held no office, made little money, and worked hard all their lives.

Some groups, women and minorities in particular, had to vault legal barriers and public hostility in order to make their contributions to the American dream, only to find that school courses taught little about their achievements. The valiant struggle of minorities and women to win dignity, equality, and justice often was omitted from history's account. Some believe this omission was accidental or careless, others insist it was purposeful.

Native Americans struggled valiantly to survive military and cultural assaults on their lives. But the public was told Native Americans were savages undeserving of any rights to their land or culture. African Americans battled to break the chains of slavery and to scale the walls of racial discrimination. But a century after slavery ended, some textbooks still pictured African Americans as content under slavery and bewildered by freedom. Arrivals from Asia, Mexico, and the West Indies faced legal restrictions and sometimes violence. But the public was told that they were undeserving of a welcome because they took "American jobs," and some were "treacherous aliens."

Whether single, married, or mothers, women were portrayed as dependent on men and accepting of a lowly status. The record of their sturdy labors, enduring strengths, and their arduous struggle to achieve equality rarely found its way into classrooms. The version of American history that reached the public carried many prejudices. It often preferred farmers over urban workers, middle classes over working classes, rich over poor. Women and minorities became invisible, ineffective, or voiceless.

This distorted legacy also failed to mention the campaigns waged by minorities and women to attain human rights. Such efforts did not reflect glory on white male rulers and their unwillingness to extend democracy and opportunity to others.

This kind of history was not a trustworthy tale. It locked out entire races and impeded racial understanding. Not only was it unreliable, but for most students it was dull and boring.

Our history has to be truthful and complete. Our struggle to overcome the barriers of nature and obstacles made by humans is an inspiring story. This series of books seeks to explore the heroic efforts of minorities and women to find their place in the American dream.

William Loren Katz

CHAPTER 1

FREEDOM SUMMER

"Free by '63." The National Association for the Advancement of Colored People (NAACP) announced its goal of having all African Americans free and equal American citizens by 1963. In August 1963, the March on Washington brought a quarter of a million people to the Lincoln Memorial to demand a civil rights law and more jobs. Dr. Martin Luther King, Jr., electrified the audience with his famous "I have a dream" speech. However, in 1963 most people of color in the South did not attend schools with whites. Nor could they enjoy a cup of coffee at a lunch counter. African Americans in the United States, except for a token few, could not get decent jobs or expect normal advances up the ladder of success.

A struggle remained, and sometimes it was violent. On a Sunday morning two weeks after the March on Washington, a bomb exploded at the 16th Street Baptist Church in Birmingham, Alabama, killing four little girls. Only a few minutes earlier they had been singing "The Love that Forgives." African Americans surged into the streets to protest this senseless violence. Within a few hours two more black men in the city had been shot and killed.

African Americans also felt a special loss with the assassination of President John F. Kennedy in Dallas, Texas, in November 1963. At first, President Kennedy had been reluctant to support the civil

A Mississippi "Freedom School" meets outdoors in 1964.

rights movement, but he was forced by events to call for a new civil rights law. He also came to symbolize a new generation of whites who saw racism as a moral cancer that had to be removed from American society. When Vice President Lyndon Johnson of Texas succeeded Kennedy, he called for passage of the civil rights bill as a tribute to the late president.

Robert Moses

As Congress debated the civil rights bill, the Student Nonviolent Coordinating Committee (SNCC) sent its "field secretaries" to help African Americans in Mississippi register to vote. The SNCC's Bob Moses, a Harlem teacher, had been a civil rights activist in Mississippi since 1961. By 1963, Moses and others were preparing entire communities to register and vote. They also helped local people further their education by establishing Freedom Schools.

However, local African Americans constantly faced death threats and violence. Churches were routinely bombed, and local African American activists disappeared. Until a new civil rights law

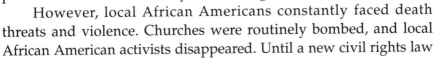

Septima Clark, the Forerunner

The "Freedom Schools" that sprouted in Mississippi in 1964 began with the efforts of teacher Septima Clark who was born in 1898. Clark began her career as an educator on Johns Island off the South Carolina coast where she lived. Many of the children and adults she knew could not read and write, so she decided to open a school. She knew many whites objected to the education of African Americans of any age, so she hid her classrooms in the back of a grocery store.

Clark's school was filled to capacity with children during the daylight hours and with adults at night. To improve their lives, Clark said, African Americans had to take part in elections. She taught adults to read so they could pass voter registration tests.

Clark finally took a job with the uniquely interracial Highlander School in Tennessee, which trained its students to combat bigotry through nonviolence. She journeyed from Virginia to Texas setting up Citizenship Schools to train people to read, write, and learn what was needed to vote. One of her most important tasks was to teach her students how to deal with white supremacists who dominated the election system.

The Freedom Schools of the 1960s grew out of Septima Clark's pioneering efforts. Some civil rights activists called her the "Mother of the Civil Rights Movement." Clark died in 1987 in her home on Johns Island, South Carolina. She had done all that she could to help her people and to advance democracy in the United States. ■

was enacted, broadening the federal government's powers to intervene, federal officials said they could not arrest the criminals. The SNCC feared that as long as the victims were local black people, the media would hardly notice the violence.

Moses, with help from Allard Lowenstein, a Jewish American attorney with a large following among white college students, devised a plan for a Mississippi "Freedom Summer." The SNCC would recruit and train college students to assist in voter registration and in Freedom Schools in Mississippi. The presence of these middle-class white students, Moses and Lowenstein reasoned, would either halt the violence or force the federal government to confront the segregationist authorities who condoned it. Nevertheless, some SNCC leaders felt that sending whites into Mississippi could undermine plans to strengthen local black leaders.

About a thousand college students — 85 percent of them middle-class whites — volunteered from a score of universities and were trained in nonviolence in a special school in Oxford, Ohio. The recruits for Mississippi were assigned to educational and voter registration projects in efforts to prepare adults and children for full participation in their citizenship. The SNCC ordered the volunteers not to test segregation laws or challenge lawmen.

People of various cultural backgrounds joined the "Freedom Summer." Abe Osherof, a Jewish American who had fought with the Lincoln Brigade in Spain, used his engineering skills to help African Americans build a rural community center. Sally Belfrage helped train women and men to take voter registration tests. She later wrote *Freedom Summer*, a vivid account of the problems young white volunteers faced during the summer of 1963.

Tragedy struck just as the first students arrived in Mississippi. On June 20 Andrew Goodman, a Jewish American youth of 21 from New York, reached Mississippi with the first 300 volunteers. He was assigned to work with black Mississippian James Chaney, 21, and Michael Schwerner, 24, another Jewish student from New York. Klansmen had decided to make an example of Schwerner to frighten away other college students.

The next day the three young men traveled to Meridian, Mississippi, to investigate a church bombing. They were arrested and held in the Neshoba County jail. When released at dark, they

FREEDOM REGISTRATION

A voter registration pamphlet that explains the process to Mississippians.

In Philadelphia, Mississippi, the FBI discovered the bodies of the three young civil rights workers.

rode off and were intercepted by two cars of armed men. The three young men were executed by the mob and buried.

The nation was shocked at their disappearance. It took 400 FBI agents and other investigators until August 4 to locate the bodies, which had been buried on a farm outside of Philadelphia, Mississippi. Searchers also found the bodies of three African Americans who had vanished. Civil rights leader Ella Baker said,

> The unfortunate thing is that it took this… to make the rest of the country turn its eyes on the the fact that there were other bodies lying under the swamps of Mississippi. Until the killing of a black mother's son becomes as important as the killing of a white mother's son, we who believe in freedom cannot rest.

Before 1964 ended, 15 African Americans had died, 33 churches had been bombed, and scores of civil rights workers had been beaten and jailed. The county sheriff, his deputy, and 19 others stood trial for the murder of Chancy, Goodman, and Schwerner but were acquitted by a white jury. A federal court then tried the suspects on civil rights violations and convicted seven men.

The brave volunteers who came to Mississippi in the next few years accomplished much but lived in fear. Young Alice Walker, a budding writer of African ancestry, taught children and adults about their historic legacies in Africa and the New World.

An interracial Mississippi Freedom Democratic Party (MFDP) emerged from the "Freedom Summer." Ella Baker and Fannie Lou Hamer, a former sharecropper, recruited courageous whites and Blacks for the party. In August 1964 Hamer led MFDP delegates to the Democratic National Convention where they demanded seating as delegates to replace the all-white Mississippi delegation. Hubert Humphrey, President Johnson's choice for vice president, offered Hamer and the MFDP a compromise — two at-large seats, having no connection with any Mississippi district, but Hamer turned this compromise down. The MFDP insisted that, as an interracial delegation, it represented all Mississippians and was pledged to support the party's stand on civil rights. A nationwide audience heard Mrs. Hamer describe her experiences with racial brutality in Mississippi. Hamer and her delegation had strong support from many northern states but were not seated. Though the MFDP lost its fight in 1964, at the next convention in 1968 the Democratic Party ruled that racially mixed delegations could not be excluded.

As FBI agents were searching Mississippi for Chaney, Goodman, and Schwerner, the most comprehensive civil rights bill in American history passed Congress. It outlawed discrimination in public accommodations and employment throughout the United States, and it permitted the attorney general to institute suits on behalf of victims of discrimination. To insure enforcement, the law directed the government to deny funds to local agencies and school systems that discriminated. When the bill passed, less than 25 percent of African American children attended desegregated schools in 11 southern states.

Democracy also advanced in 1964 with passage of the 24th Amendment to the Constitution which eliminated poll taxes. Since 1866, many of the South's poor had been kept from voting by poll taxes. Black voting demands were decisive in this victory.

CHAPTER 2

THE BACKLASH

The civil rights movement was only beginning to accomplish its objectives when it faced a white counteroffensive. This counteroffensive was called a "white backlash." However, African American leaders saw the "backlash" as part of an old pattern. They pointed out that every time African Americans tried to advance themselves, some white Americans became stubborn or violent. The Ku Klux Klan had been part of a white backlash that had lasted for a hundred years.

In 1964 Governor George Wallace of Alabama decided openly to test the political weight of the backlash vote by entering three state Democratic Party presidential primaries as the white man's candidate. In Wisconsin he won 34 percent of the vote, in Indiana 30 percent, and in Maryland 43 percent. Clearly the backlash had voting clout.

Klan cross-burning in Maryland in May 1966.

The white backlash also operated on more subtle levels than noisy Klansmen and racist candidates. Many whites responded to the black presence in cities by moving to the suburbs. Major cities gained black residents and lost whites. When urban schools integrated, most whites remained as long as they were in a clear majority. But when the black student population reached the 40 percent level, many white parents moved their children to private or parochial schools, or to suburban districts. Few African Americans could afford to do the same.

Jeering white youths in 1967 in Milwaukee, WI, disrupt an "Open Housing" march by white and black marchers.

In 1966 Dr. King decided to bring his crusade for integrated housing to Chicago. When he led his marchers into white neighborhoods, it took 2,000 police to hold back the screaming, bottle-throwing crowds. Some held signs reading, "We Need a Ku Klux Klan." King, who was hit by a rock, said, "I think the people of Mississippi ought to come to Chicago to learn how to hate."

Many of the white men and women who taunted King's marchers were descendants of European immigrants who had been successful enough to settle in the suburbs. They viewed African Americans as "inferiors" and examples of the poverty they had fled. They also feared that Blacks would take their jobs.

King also received support from sons and daughters of European immigrants. John Rossen, a Jewish American, marched with Dr. King into Cicero, Illinois, along with Catholic priests, Protestant ministers, and other Jews. In Milwaukee, Wisconsin, Father James Groppi, the son of an Italian immigrant, led African Americans and whites for three weeks in "Open Housing" marches. The National Guard had to hold back mobs of angry white men, some of whom wore swastikas.

Meanwhile, another backlash to the movement had developed inside the Federal Justice Department. On the day of the March on Washington, FBI Director J. Edgar Hoover decided that King and his followers were "under Communist control." Hoover had no proof of this, but he had the power to act on his belief. He sent FBI agents to disrupt the legal activities of civil rights groups. President Lyndon Johnson authorized the FBI use of wiretaps against the MFDP at the Democratic Party convention in 1964 and also approved wiretaps on Dr. King. Under the guise of fighting Communist subversion in the United States, Hoover ordered his FBI agents to infiltrate and disrupt a vast number of American reform and protest organizations.

Hoover's actions had far-reaching and grave consequences for individuals and American civil liberties. FBI agents not only spied on private groups in violation of their constitutional rights but hampered their communications and pitted one leader against another. Through such tactics, Hoover's agents had virtually destroyed the American Communist Party by 1956. Now they carried their campaign into groups unrelated to communism or subversion.

Martin Luther King, Jr., and his wife Coretta in the 1965 march from Selma to Montgomery, Alabama.

On March 7, 1965, Dr. King, John Lewis of the SNCC, and Hosea Williams of the Southern Christian Leadership Conference (SCLC) planned a 50-mile march from Selma, Alabama, to Montgomery to demand black voting rights in Alabama. White tempers rose. Even before the march started, two civil rights activists, Jimmie Lee Jackson, an African American youth, and James Reeb, a white Boston minister, who had been assisting in voter registration, were slain by racists.

Nevertheless, 500 marchers under Lewis and Williams began their march across the Edmund Pettus Bridge in Selma toward Montgomery. Alabama state troopers blocked their way and then threw tear gas cannisters at the lead column. Troopers chased and beat fleeing marchers with clubs and whips. Sheyann Webb, who was eight years old at the time, remembered: "I saw people being beaten, and I tried to run home as fast as I could." Williams began to carry the girl, but Webb told him to put her down because "he wasn't running fast enough."

Dr. Bunche Marches

Striding forward in the front ranks of the Selma marchers in 1965 was Dr. Ralph Bunche, a man who had made his mark not as a civil rights activist but as a scholar and diplomat. His presence was symbolic of the support major African American figures in the cultural, sports, and entertainment arenas provided for Dr. Martin Luther King's crusade.

Bunche was born poor in Detroit in 1904, the grandson of a slave. When his parents died, his grandmother moved the family to Los Angeles where the young man attended Jefferson High School and graduated from UCLA in 1927. Then Bunche attended Harvard University on a college tuition scholarship that was supplemented by money raised by African American women's clubs.

For years Dr. Bunche served as an assistant to Swedish scholar, Gunnar Myrdal, who was completing a huge study of American racial relations called *An American Dilemma* (1944). During World War II, Bunche worked for the State Department.

In 1946 Bunche became a United Nations official. Replacing an assassinated UN mediator in 1948, he worked tirelessly to bring peace to the Arab-Israeli conflict. In 1950 he was awarded the Nobel Peace Prize, becoming the second American at that time to win the prize. After many years as a top UN official, Dr. Bunche died in 1971. ■

This "Bloody Sunday" on the bridge in Selma reached a shocked world on TV. When Dr. King tried to lead another march two days later, state troopers at the bridge again halted it. King, fearing a price in blood to his followers, ended the march.

President Johnson then told a nationwide TV audience that America "must overcome the crippling legacy of bigotry and injustice." He asked Congress for a new voting rights law with enforcement powers. Adopting the theme of the civil rights movement, he said, "We shall overcome." Johnson had committed himself to the goals of the civil rights movement. For the white Texan president it was, perhaps, his most triumphant moment.

A federal court ruled that Dr. King and his followers must be allowed to march. Thousands of Americans came to join him — Catholic nuns, Protestant ministers, representatives of Jewish groups, Native Americans, and many other citizens appalled at the burden African Americans had to bear for demanding the vote. President Johnson federalized the Alabama National Guard and had them escort the marchers from Selma to Montgomery. He also sent along federal troops, marshals, and FBI agents.

The 25,000 marchers who reached Montgomery included Dr. Ralph Bunche, Roy Wilkins, A. Philip Randolph, Bayard Rustin, and Stokely Carmichael. John Lewis walked along, his head still bandaged from his Pettus Bridge beating. The crowd assembled before the State Capitol and heard Dr. King ask for a new era of human rights in Alabama. "The road ahead is not altogether a smooth one," he warned his audience. "There are no broad highways to lead us easily and inevitably to quick solutions."

On the last day of the march, murder struck on the highway from Selma. Mrs. Viola Liuzzo, an Italian American housewife from Detroit, was assassinated by a car full of Ku Klux Klan members as she drove marchers home.

The violence continued during that summer in Lowndes County, Alabama, where a white Protestant seminarian was killed and a white Catholic priest was mortally wounded. Both had been helping in voter registration campaigns. By the end of 1965, 108 men and women had died for civil rights since 1955.

President Johnson, like President Kennedy, had preferred to work for change peacefully and "behind the scenes" and to avoid conflicts between state and federal officials. But, like Kennedy, Johnson had been pushed by the momentum of events.

In Johnson's 1965 Voting Rights Act, Congress eliminated almost all qualifying tests for voting and made the federal government the final arbitrator of whether a voter's rights had been violated. Federal officials began to arrive in the South to assist in the registration of voters, and by 1966, more than half of eligible African Americans in 11 southern states were registered to vote. The following year members of the MFDP were elected sheriffs, school board members, and to other local posts.

The Voting Rights Act also opened political avenues for people who did not speak English. It eliminated state literacy tests that had long kept Mexican Americans, Puerto Ricans, and others whose first language was Spanish from being able to register and vote. The new law allowed citizens to register if they had earned an elementary school diploma in a country where the classroom language was not English. Within five years Puerto Ricans in New York elected their first representative to Congress and sent four others to the state legislature. In the Southwest, politicians realized they now had to court Mexican American voters.

But the laws of 1964 and 1965 did not stop racial murders. In January 1965, Sammy Younge Jr., 22, a black college student, was slain for attempting to use a white restroom at a gas station in Tuskegee, Alabama. A week later Vernon Dahmer, an African American civil rights leader, was slain in Hattiesburg, Mississippi.

In June 1966, James Meredith, who had integrated the University of Mississippi four years earlier, singlehandedly began a "march against fear" in Mississippi. He hoped to spur black courage and voter registration in the state. On the second day of his march, surrounded by FBI agents, Meredith was shot from ambush. As Meredith recovered in a hospital, Dr. King, Roy Wilkins, and other civil rights figures promised to complete his march. King led a prayer service for the slain Chaney, Schwerner, and Goodman on the steps of the Neshoba County courthouse. He quoted the words of an old spiritual when he said, "Before I'll be a slave, I will be dead in my grave." Nearby white Mississippians shouted "We'll help you!" and heaved bottles and rocks at the marchers.

As the "Meredith March" walked along a Mississippi highway, a new figure emerged. The SNCC's new chairman, Stokely Carmichael, 24, had graduated from Howard University and had been arrested 27 times for civil rights activities. Believing in self-defense, he urged the marchers to accept protection from the Deacons for Defense and Justice, a black Louisiana group that carried loaded weapons. Dr. King accepted their aid but had them leave their guns at home.

Marchers made their way through rural Mississippi where Blacks had lived under a despotic government for generations. To local people who came out to greet the marchers, Carmichael shouted, "Black Power!" Some people appeared to like that slogan better than King's "Freedom Now!" At one point marchers were met by white mobs, and both sides fired at each other. A new phase of the civil rights revolution had begun.

BLACK POWER

The message of Black Power that Stokely Carmichael proclaimed in 1965 had a prior history. It was first voiced by Malcolm X. Born Malcolm Little in Omaha, Nebraska, in 1925, to a father who had been a follower of black nationalist figure Marcus Garvey, Malcolm's father died when Malcolm was still a boy. The young man grew up believing his father died because of his support for Garvey.

Malcolm Little reached the eighth grade and then left for New York City where as "Big Red" he worked as a waiter in Harlem. At 21 he was arrested for burglary and sentenced to ten years in prison. In jail he spent his time studying African American history. He also became a follower of the Nation of Islam religion and its leader, the Honorable Elijah Muhammad.

In 1963 civil rights leader Malcolm X addressed a rally in Harlem, New York, supporting desegregation marches in Birmingham, Alabama.

The Black Muslims said whites were devils and African Americans should separate themselves from the evil in white society. Like his fellow Black Muslims, Malcolm saw his last name as a relic of days when masters named their slaves. He changed it to Malcolm X.

Discharged from prison in 1952, Malcolm became a leader of the Black Muslims and, for 12 years, the spokesperson and chief assistant to Elijah Muhammad. A gifted orator and teacher, Malcolm's impact was immediate in many communities. He challenged racism as a system founded on violence and called on African Americans to take pride in their color and defend themselves when necessary from all enemies, even the police. Malcolm called for a united front by people of African descent living throughout the world.

To those who urged integration as the solution to racism, he answered, "I'd rather be dead than integrated into the American nightmare." His message to his people was one of hope, unity, and determination. He never advocated violence but told his people they "were crazy to be nonviolent as long as your enemies practice violence on you."

Centuries of oppression, Malcolm said, had spawned deep-rooted feelings of inferiority in people of color. He insisted that this sense of inferiority had to be uprooted in order to win the fight for equality and justice. He reminded his people that American Jews had pooled their economic resources, helped one another as family, and had united to battle anti-Semitism.

Because Malcolm said African Americans had a right to resist oppression "by any means necessary," critics tried to contrast his approach to the nonviolence of Dr. King. The two men, however, agreed on many important issues, particularly as Malcolm's philosophy matured.

In 1964, after Malcolm X had left Elijah Muhammad because of a series of disagreements, he visited African and Asian nations to pray and talk with Muslims of many colors. This experience made a great impact on him, and he redefined his approach: "Hating white men did not bring us anything." He said,

> If you attack him because he is white, you give him no out. He can't stop being white. We've got to give the man a chance.

Though seen as foes by the press, in March 1964 Dr. King and Malcolm X had a friendly discussion and posed for pictures.

In Africa Malcolm accidentally met SNCC representatives. This led to planned meetings with civil rights activists. He formed an Organization of Afro-American Unity. He also began to speak of "human rights" and to argue for "Black Nationalism," which would later be called Black Power. His point was that African American communities had to control the institutions and policies that affected them. They had to shape their own affairs free of outside interference. Black people, he said, first had to unite among themselves before they joined with others. "Whites can help us," he said, "but they can't join us."

Malcolm still said that it was "criminal to teach a man not to defend himself when he is the constant victim of brutal attacks."

People should remain law-abiding, he said, but be prepared to fight back until the government starts "doing its job."

Malcolm feared violent retaliation from the followers of Elijah Muhammad. He had received many death threats, and once his home was bombed. Still he continued speaking in public. "He believed," his wife Betty Shabazz said later, that the federal government "would have him killed but would use the Black Muslims."

During a talk at the Audubon Ballroom in Harlem, New York, on February 21, 1965, before a crowd that included his wife and four young daughters, Malcolm was assassinated by three Black Muslims. The assassins fired 16 shots into him, and he died almost immediately.

At his funeral Malcolm was eulogized by actor and civil rights activist Ossie Davis as "our own shining black prince, Malcolm was our manhood, our living black manhood!" At his grave African American mourners refused to let white gravediggers bury him. The mourners themselves, some with shovels and others with handfuls of earth, buried Malcolm X.

Malcolm's legacy and teachings about pride and self-assertion inspired millions of people. He was part of a rising generation that called on African American people to end their fear, study their history, and stand up and be counted in the world.

Stokely Carmichael, who became chairman of the SNCC, had studied the ideas of Malcolm X and expressed them with his Black Power slogan. He explained that "Black Power" meant that African American communities had to pursue their own agenda. They had to run their own schools, businesses, and political organizations. He did not see a peaceful end to racism and offered this view:

In 1967 Stokely Carmichael was photographed by Gordon Parks in Alabama.

> Each time the [African American] people in those cities saw Martin Luther King get slapped, they became angry; when they saw four little black girls bombed to death [in Birmingham] they were angrier; and when nothing happened, they were steaming.

There were many reactions to Black Power within African American communities. Ella Baker said that the SNCC turned to Black Power out of a sense of frustration with American democracy. Black Southerners had risked their lives and still lacked protection by their government. White America was moving too slowly toward equality, and some people refused to move at all. Black college students, she said, believed the government they had been taught to admire in class had failed to work for their people, so they chose "a more revolutionary approach."

Carmichael explained Black Power as the ability of black communities to pick black police, own their banks, insurance companies and stores, and run their own schools. "When the whole city of Harlem is run by Blacks," said one follower of Carmichael, "then you have some Black Power."

The media made Carmichael's Black Power slogan appear to be an invitation to violence. In several cities, police raided SNCC headquarters and arrested staff members. FBI agents began to trail Carmichael and SNCC officials and disrupt their activities.

In 1967, H. Rap Brown, another civil rights activist, replaced Carmichael as chairman of the SNCC. Brown took part in a demonstration in Orangeburg, South Carolina, in which the National Guard fired at college students killing four and injuring 33. The SNCC lost members after Brown visited Communist countries and adopted some of their slogans and ideas.

Black Power also divided civil rights figures. Roy Wilkins of the NAACP predicted that it would "lead to black death." Dr. Kenneth Clark predicted it would bring "the very segregation we have been fighting all these years." Dr. King said he did not favor any program that excluded white people from the black liberation effort. Eventually Dr. King's SCLC and the Urban League accepted the SNCC's basic idea of empowering people of color to run their own communities.

Some African American leaders of the SNCC urged whites to leave. They wanted to replace older white leaders with younger black ones who used Black Power's language of defiance. The SNCC lost old members, particularly whites, and began to have trouble raising funds to continue their activities. Many white journalists began to compare Black Power to Klan violence.

In December 1966, a SNCC staff meeting debated becoming a black nationalist organization and excluding whites entirely. Carmichael agreed with the proposals, but James Forman and Fannie Lou Hamer did not, and the vote was 19 to 18 to remain interracial. The 24 whites present did not vote and left the SNCC meeting feeling discouraged.

H. Rap Brown urged whites who had helped in civil rights efforts to return to their own communities and fight the racism they found. But few took up his suggestion to fight white supremacy.

In Newark, New Jersey, in 1967, over a thousand people converged from 26 states, 126 cities, and 286 different groups for the first Black Power Conference. A new breed of leaders stepped into the limelight including Ron Karenga, James Farmer, and Jesse Jackson. Their resolution read:

> Black people who live under the racist governments of America, Asia, Africa, and Latin America stand at the crossroads of either an expanding revolution or ruthless extermination. It is incumbent on us to get our house in order, if we are fully to utilize the potentialities of the revolution, or to resist our own execution.
>
> Black people have consistently expended a large part of our energy and resources reacting to white definition. It is imperative that we begin to develop the organizational and technical competence to initiate and enact our own programs.

The Black Power movement soon had its own flag of red, green, and black. African American dress and hairstyles began to reflect those in Africa. Black Power offered a new sense of racial pride, a potent feeling that when people of color stood together they could not be defeated.

Beginning with the new country of Ghana in 1957, African nations began to smash the chains of European colonialism. Many

The 1967 Newark Black Power conference brought together many activists, including Ron Karenga, H. Rap Brown, Jesse Jackson, and others.

Black Power in History

Black Power was not a new idea or new slogan. It frequently was expressed by African American communities during times of intense oppression or great opportunity. Its creator was Martin R. Delany, a Harvard-educated medical man who awoke each morning proud to be "a black man." He visited Africa searching for a homeland for African Americans. In 1859 Delany signed an agreement with a Nigerian king, but nothing came of his plan. Afterward he became a major during the Civil War and a politician in South Carolina. He believed that "Black men must have black leaders."

Reverend Henry McNeal Turner, the first black chaplain in the Civil War, also believed in black pride and a return to Africa, and said, "God is black." In 1896, Turner said the African American should

> build up a nation of his own, and create a language in keeping with his color, as the whites have done. Nor will he ever respect himself until he does it.

In 1899 Sutton Griggs wrote a novel that advocated an African American conspiracy to capture Texas and Louisiana during wartime, and keep Texas as a black state. In the 1920s Marcus Garvey stirred millions of African Americans with his message of black liberation throughout Africa and the world. And just days before Stokely Carmichael called for Black Power in 1966, Harlem congressman Adam Clayton Powell used these words, calling on African Americans to stand up for themselves.

Beginning in the 1930s, the Black Muslims, a religious sect led by Elijah Muhammad, advocated building an economically independent African American community, separate from white law, police, and government. By 1975, when Elijah Muhammad died, the Black Muslims, had 160,000 members and operated businesses and schools. ■

In 1964 Congressman Adam Clayton Powell (center) was photographed with Malcolm X (right) and Reverend Milton Galemison (left).

African leaders drew inspiration and lessons from the African American civil rights and Black Power movements. And many African Americans were thrilled by the new independent nations of Africa.

CHAPTER 4

THE BLACK PANTHERS

Stokely Carmichael's SNCC was not the only organization in the United States encouraging Blacks to take charge of their own destiny. At about the same time Stokely Carmichael shouted about Black Power in Mississippi and Alabama, the Black Panther Party for Self-Defense was organized in Oakland, California, by Huey Newton and Bobby Seale.

Newton, born in 1942 in Louisiana, moved to California with his family, attended Merritt College, and took classes at a law school. He also took courses at a music conservatory and mastered the concert piano. Seale, born in Dallas, Texas, in 1936, moved to California with his family, served in the air force, and then graduated from high school. He became a carpenter, a sheet metalworker, and a musician.

Members of the Black Panther Party study The Little Red Book, *which contains the saying of Communist leader Mao Tse-tung.*

When they met at Merritt College, the two young men found they had much in common. Both Newton and Seale were members of the pro-nationalist Afro-American Association and both demanded black history courses and more black instructors. But they became disappointed with the association's narrow antiwhite approach.

The two men took jobs at the North Oakland Poverty Center and began to canvass Oakland's African American neighborhoods, asking residents what they needed and wanted. They also began to read revolutionary writers, such as Malcolm X, and Marxists writers, including Mao Tse-tung, Ho Chi Minh, and Che Guevara.

Newton and Seale formed the Black Panther Party (BPP) to continue Malcolm X's Organization of Afro-American Unity. Their heroes were leaders of slave rebellions — Denmark Vesey, Gabriel Prosser, and Nat Turner.

The Black Panthers focused their attention on basic ghetto problems. They viewed the police as an unwelcome army of occupation too willing to use unnecessary force. Since California law permitted the carrying of unconcealed weapons, the Panthers kept watch in cars filled with rifles and law books. Their patrols trailed the police and observed arrest procedures. Complaints of police brutality began to decline in the neighborhoods they patrolled.

White reporters portrayed the Panthers as gun-toting former convicts turned revolutionaries. While some early recruits had been criminals, they had to reform or leave the Panthers. The Panthers soon stimulated pride among many ghetto residents.

J. Edgar Hoover ordered the FBI to infiltrate the BPP from top to bottom. Never before had African Americans formed an armed organization to promote their own revolutionary beliefs.

Actually, most Panther programs focused not on revolution but on local issues. The BPP protested rent evictions, helped welfare recipients, offered courses in black history, and campaigned for traffic lights at dangerous school crossings. Their most popular and successful campaign was to provide free breakfasts for schoolchildren. They found that pupils in ghetto neighborhoods came to class too hungry to concentrate on their lessons.

White dread rose as Panthers criticized American capitalism and its crusade against world communism. When 30 armed Panthers, including six women, appeared at California's state capitol to protest a gun-control bill, they became front-page news. Fear of the Panthers led white legislators to pass the gun-control bill. But this publicity helped to create new BPP clubs in Georgia, Tennessee, Los Angeles, Detroit, and New York.

Oakland police and the FBI planned to silence the Panthers and eliminate their leaders. In October 1967, Huey Newton was in his van when he was stopped by a police car in the early morning. As he got out of his van, shooting erupted. A police officer was slain and Newton was shot four times in the stomach. Newton was jailed without bail and charged with murder.

A "Free Huey" campaign reached from coast to coast. During his trial for murder, Newton denied that he had fired at anyone when he was cut down by police bullets. Despite contradictory evidence, Newton was found guilty and received a sentence of 2 to 15 years in jail. His conviction was reversed when an appeals court found major trial errors. By the time he was released, Newton had served two years in prison.

In California, radicals of both races formed a Peace and Freedom Party that allied itself with the Panthers. The SNCC and the Panthers also drew together but found they did not agree about making alliances with whites. The Panthers favored these alliances, and SNCC members were opposed.

The next year Panther leader Eldridge Cleaver ran for president of the United States on the Peace and Freedom Party ticket and received an estimated 200,000 votes. Panther chapters had now sprouted in cities from coast to coast. The media caricatured Panthers as revolutionaries in black leather jackets, black pants, and black berets who waved weapons and shouted slogans, but to many people who lived in ghettoes, the BPP meant hope and power.

By 1968, the FBI had drawn up careful plans to throttle the Panthers. That year President Johnson gave J. Edgar Hoover permission to expand his secret counterintelligence program, COINTELPRO, to include surveillance of the Panthers and other "Black Nationalist groups." Hoover publicly denounced the Panthers as "the greatest threat to the internal security of the country." He ordered his secret agents to "exploit all avenues of creating… dissension within the ranks of the BPP." Police raided BPP headquarters, and many leaders were jailed.

FBI agents used forged letters to pit the Panthers against the Blackstone Rangers, a rival armed group based in Chicago that the Panthers were about to unite with. Two days after the murder of Dr. King the police raided a Panther meeting in Oakland. Member Bobby Hutton was shot and killed with his hands in the air. Cleaver was wounded and arrested.

In 1968, after being implicated in a shooting incident, Cleaver fled the country. He was welcomed in Arab nations and in Cuba, countries hostile to the United States.

In 1968 Black Panther leader Eldridge Cleaver fled the country, and the FBI issued this "wanted" notice.

In 1966 Black Panthers used a theater party to raise money in New York City.

Meanwhile, the law enforcement conflict with the Panthers continued to take a heavy toll. In December 1969, Seale's attorney, Charles Garry, told reporters that 28 Panthers had been killed by the police. The American Civil Liberties Union stated that law enforcement officials had declared war against the BPP.

In Chicago in 1969, the FBI and local police plotted to destroy the Panther's hold on a local Chicago community. On December 4, 1969, using floor plans supplied by FBI informant William O'Neal, a high Panther Party official, 14 police officers raided the apartment of Fred Hampton in the early morning when everyone was asleep. At 21, Hampton was a charismatic BPP figure in his ghetto community. He and Panther Fred Clark were killed in their beds, and four other members were wounded. There were no police casualties. The police claimed they fired in self-defense, but later evidence proved that no shots had come from within the apartment. Hampton was apparently slain at close range while asleep. Though the FBI and police tried to cover up their actions, a court later awarded the families of Hampton and Clark almost $2 million in compensation. By this time, however, the power of the Black Panther Party had been smashed.

Fred Hampton, chairman of the Illinois Black Panthers, speaks at a rally in Chicago.

The Young Lords

In 1968, young Puerto Rican Americans in New York City's East Harlem *barrio* formed the Young Lords. Patterned after the Black Panthers, its members also wanted rapid social change.

In 1970, Young Lords, dressed in black leather jackets and berets, seized a church to persuade its leaders to be more supportive of the community. Like the Panthers they shouted "Power to the People" and ran community self-help projects such as youth clubs,

drug rehabilitation centers, school breakfast programs, and health clinics. Because of their military dress and flamboyant manner, they also attracted police and FBI surveillance. However, their aim was not to promote violence or revolution but to instill ethnic pride in Puerto Ricans.

Mexican American youths in California formed Brown Berets clubs. They tried to organize programs similar to those of the Black Panthers. ■

CHAPTER 5

THE WAR IN VIETNAM

The war in Southeast Asia increasingly gained American public attention in the 1960s. At first most Americans supported the war as part of the struggle against world communism. Then many among the young and minorities began to question if the war was about communism or even if American national interests were being threatened. In 1965, McComb's Mississippi Freedom Democratic Party became the first group to denounce the war and call for young men "not to honor the draft here in Mississippi."

The country became bitterly divided when President Johnson escalated the number of American troops in Vietnam. This action diverted funds from his War on Poverty just as it was getting under way. Some young men who faced the draft left for Canada or sought college deferments. In 1966 African American state representative Julian Bond was denied his seat in the Georgia legislature for opposing the war. The Supreme Court ordered him reinstated.

World heavyweight champion Muhammad Ali was stripped of his heavyweight championship for saying he would not be drafted into the U.S. Army. He said,

> No, I am not going 10,000 miles to help murder and kill and burn other people simply to help continue the domination of white slave masters over the dark people the world over.

In 1967 Dr. Martin Luther King, Jr., spoke for many, particularly young people, when he denounced the war. He called the United States "the greatest purveyor of violence in the world today" and told young men not to register for the

Champion boxer Muhammad Ali (Cassius Clay) shown with Elijah Muhammad of the powerful Nation of Islam.

draft. King now stressed far more than the civil rights of African Americans:

> The black revolution is much more than a struggle for the rights of Negroes. It is forcing America to face all its interrelated flaws — racism, poverty, militarism, and materialism. It is exposing the evils that are rooted deeply in the whole structure of our society. It reveals systemic rather than superficial flaws and suggests that radical reconstruction of society itself is the real issue to be faced.

In 1967 King and Stokely Carmichael led an antiwar parade to the United Nations. "Hell, no, we won't go," shouted Carmichael into the microphone. The huge crowd made it a chant.

In the late 1960s and early 1970s, many young men and women attacked American foreign policy and called for solidarity with the oppressed of the world. People of color linked their demand for self-determination with demands that American aid be cancelled for foreign rulers who opposed colonial liberation or promoted white supremacy. A Chicano youth said,

The U.S. Army was fully integrated during the Vietnam War.

> The struggle of our *barrios* is the struggle of the whole world. And the only way to win liberation for our people is by uniting with other oppressed people.

In 1970, 10,000 Chicanos in Los Angeles marched to protest the Vietnam War. They were attacked by police, and three Chicanos died, including Lyn War, a girl of 15. Rioting by Chicanos erupted in the city.

People of color were often overrepresented among the American troops sent to Vietnam, particularly among the dead and wounded. In 1966 black servicemen made up more than 22 percent of those killed in action, double their percentage in the population. Men with Spanish surnames constituted 11 percent of the population but 19 percent of the casualties in Vietnam.

28

Native Americans used the Vietnam War to assert their independence from U.S. foreign policy. Sid Mills, a Yakima and Cherokee Indian, served for two years and four months in Vietnam and was critically wounded. He said,

> I owe and swear my first allegiance to Indian People in the sovereign rights of our many Tribes. Owing to this allegiance and the commitment it now draws me to, I hereby renounce further obligation in service or duty to the United States Army....
>
> My decision is influenced by the fact that we have already buried Indian fishermen returned dead from Vietnam, while Indian fishermen live here without protection and under steady attack from… this Nation and the states of Washington and Oregon.

In 1970 Manuel Gomez, a Chicano, refused to honor his draft call. He responded,

> For my people, I refuse to respect your induction papers. Too many of my brothers have died fighting for a lie called "American Freedom." My people have known nothing but racist tyranny and brutal oppression from this society. For the Vietnamese people, too, I refuse.... They are not my enemy but brothers involved in the same struggle for justice against a common enemy. We are all branches of the same tree, flowers of the same garden, waves of the same sea.

Private Milton Olive died when he threw himself on a grenade to save four fellow soldiers in Vietnam in 1965.

CHAPTER 6

FROM VIETNAM TO AMERICA

The long Vietnam War created thousands of refugees. The fall of Saigon in 1975, which ended the war, resulted in a first wave of refugees comprised mainly of members of the country's ruling class. These were people who had supported American aims and thought that they would face death under the Communists. An orderly evacuation effort organized by the United States government collapsed under the weight of the number of fleeing people. Chaos ruled as people who feared for their lives tried to reach America. Television news showed scenes of frantic men and women trying to catch the last army helicopters leaving the roof of the American Embassy in Saigon.

In 1966 an interpreter hired by the U.S. Army (right) questions a mother about the location of the enemy. Many Vietnamese who served the U.S. came to America to settle when the war ended.

Desperation led people to hijack planes to U.S. bases in Thailand. Some seized rickety sailing boats at gunpoint, and still others sailed the sea on homemade floats in hopes an American ship would pick them up. By April 1975, an estimated 40,000 had fled South Vietnam, and in a few more months, 200,000.

Since the U.S. promise to halt the North Vietnamese Communists had failed, Congress felt responsible for resettling these newcomers. Vietnamese with contacts in America or who spoke English were most likely to find a home in the United States. This group was usually young, skilled, and wealthy. Three-quarters had a high school education, and 20 percent had attended college.

Reception centers for thousands of refugees were built at U.S. bases in Thailand, the Philippines, and on the American-owned islands of the Pacific. Vietnamese refugees were sent to bases in California, Arkansas, Florida, and Pennsylvania. Most arrivals were young, with 82 percent under 35. To leave a base, a refugee family had to have sponsors, people who would help them find work, a home, and schools for their children. These Vietnamese arrived in the United States as refugees, not under immigration laws. They were aided in the search for sponsors by voluntary groups such as the Catholic Conference, the Church World Service, the Lutheran Immigration and Refugee Service, the United Hebrew Immigrant Aid Society, and the American Fund for Czechoslovak Refugees.

In 1975 these South Vietnamese refugees arrived at Fort Chaffee, Arkansas, to begin the process of entering American society.

However, the newcomers confronted a serious housing problem. Rarely did sponsors take in refugee family groups of 25, the typical number for a Vietnamese extended family. Uncles, aunts, grandparents, cousins, and nephews who had lived together for years were separated as they entered the United States.

United States policy was to disperse the refugees around the country. This was partially to insure that no one local or state authority was overwhelmed. This policy of dispersal, officials also believed, would compel newcomers to adapt to American society. They felt that living with other Vietnamese would hinder the process of assimilation.

In 1980 these 326 Vietnamese boat people were rescued from the China Sea by a U.S. ship. Most came to America.

When the victorious Communist forces in Vietnam tried to force millions to live and work in the countryside, this led to a further exodus. When Vietnamese bankers, secretaries, and salespeople rejected farm work, the new government became more insistent and harsh.

The Vietnamese found their only escape was by sea. Called boat people, thousands climbed on board small fishing vessels or large cargo ships. Others made rafts from empty oil drums. Many boats held double or triple the safe number of men, women, and children. Some boats were not seaworthy. Some vessels, 20 feet by 5 feet, carried as many as 70 refugees.

The boat people included some wealthy and middle-class Vietnamese, but most were poor people with few skills and little education. Few refugees carried any possessions or money, and those that did often lost them at sea.

Perilous efforts to escape cost an estimated 40,000 to 200,000 lives, mostly people who were lost at sea. Food and water was limited and sometimes ran out. Storms tossed people over the side to watery graves. People died from starvation when boats lost their way at sea. Some refugees survived for weeks on raw rice. Finally, there was terror at sea. Pirates attacked boats to capture food, clothing, and money. However, every month as many as 14,000 boat people from Vietnam reached safety. Vietnamese women desperately tried to hold their large families together. Older brothers and sisters calmed infants and the young. Those who survived the trip spent years trying to locate loved ones who had taken other boats.

Many Asian countries rejected the boat people as an unnecessary burden on their meager resources. Thailand allowed pirates to attack the boats or drive them in another direction. Refugees who rejoiced when a cargo ship came into view found that many captains did not rescue drifting craft since ports would not accept boat people. The United States took in more boat people than all the other nations combined, and Canada was second. Church-affiliated agencies found sponsors for 89,000 people.

Life in refugee camps was not easy for the survivors. Even those who knew possible American sponsors did not know how to contact them. Refugee camps offered adults and children no work, little education, and a life of boredom.

In 1979 the United Nations and the Vietnamese government worked out an Orderly Departure Program that allowed persons accepted by another country to leave Vietnam. In America refugees were given top priority if they were "close family members." The next priority was given to Vietnamese who had worked for the U.S. government, or who could demonstrate a close tie to the United States, or who would face persecution if they remained. By 1986, 50,000 Vietnamese refugees entered America under this program.

Vietnamese refugees qualified for food stamps, Medicaid, loans, and other financial aid. After their first three years in the U.S., most no longer accepted federal financial assistance. They formed their own self-help groups in such cities as Seattle, New Orleans, and Washington, D.C. These societies helped locate lost relatives, provided English classes, and offered financial assistance. Societies also tried to preserve traditional Vietnamese cultural life.

By 1986, there were Vietnamese living in all 50 states. Texas had accepted more than 61,000, California more than 317,000, and the state of Washington more than 37,000.

Life in America posed many problems for the refugees. Vietnamese families were close, and children were taught to listen to their father at all times. However, when large families were dispersed to different locations around the country, family values were undermined. Vietnamese, accustomed to a family structure of 20 or 30 that included grandparents, aunts, and uncles, bitterly resented being separated in America.

In 1979 this Vietnamese refugee family had settled down in Washington, D.C.

The refugees, however, often solved their own problems. People sent to one city tried to link up with family members in other cities or to settle in Vietnamese neighborhoods in their assigned cities. Children found it hard to understand the independence of American boys and girls whose parents exerted less control over

In 1975 this Vietnamese refugee worked at a checkout counter in a supermarket in Washington, D.C.

them. But soon the Vietnamese began to learn new ways.

The newcomers were offered low-paying jobs that others did not want, and they had no choice but to accept them. In 1975, 85 percent of Vietnamese who once held good-paying, white-collar work had to take blue-collar jobs. Half of all wives and daughters over age 16 had to work to support their families. Many salaries were too low to support families, so people again needed federal aid.

Conflicts arose when white citizens thought the Vietnamese were taking "American jobs." In Galveston, Texas, Ku Klux Klan members claimed Vietnamese fishermen were Communists and tried to burn their boats. Some white Americans looked down on refugees who took work "no American would take."

Most boat people were Buddhists, but some were followers of Confucius, and still others believed in Taoism. Many combined the teachings of more than one religion. A minority of refugees were Catholics or belonged to other Christian religions, and some arrived with their priests or ministers. Coming from a nonintrusive culture, they resented efforts by evangelical sects to convert them.

Although the Vietnamese treasured education and respected teachers, their education stressed memorization and discipline rather than learning to think independently. Children looked to the teacher as the final authority, whereas American educators saw themselves as classroom guides encouraging children to think for themselves. Vietnamese children tried hard at school to learn the new ways. Learning English confused them. Their language has six basic tones, and the sound of each word is part of its meaning. This differs from English, which is not tonal.

Vietnamese had to make social adjustments in their manner. They bowed their heads to show respect and honor, and looked away when speaking to someone. In America these customs could cause misunderstandings. The color white represents death to

Vietnamese, so hospitals became frightening places, and weddings at first did not appear to be happy occasions.

By 1980, over a hundred Vietnamese self-help and social groups had formed in America. Cambodian and Laotian immigrants also formed their own self-help groups. In Boulder, Colorado, the Vietnamese Alliance held weekly meetings and organized volleyball and soccer games. It published a newsletter, gave advice by telephone, and helped members find jobs and homes. San Diego's Cambodian Association had 300 members, and provided emergency housing and aid in dealing with federal agencies.

Vietnamese refugees wanted to learn English, to improve their economic situation, and to become American citizens. But they also wanted to preserve their own customs and to help family members find contentment in their new homeland. By the 1980s, many refugees had become cooks, construction workers, college professors, business people, social workers, priests, computer experts, and engineers. Following in the footsteps of 19th century waves of immigrants from Europe and Asia, many started their own retail businesses. Their children quickly began to adopt the clothing and hairstyles of American teenagers.

This Vietnamese refugee ran a large Arlington, Virginia, grocery store.

CHAPTER 7

REBIRTH OF LA RAZA

The civil rights movement helped arouse strong feelings of self-identification among Mexican Americans. The most dynamic and successful Chicano leader, Cesar Chavez, was inspired by Dr. Martin Luther King, Jr. The oldest boy of six children, Chavez was born in Arizona in 1927 to the offspring of Mexican immigrants. Chavez has said his early life was poor but happy. His family lost its farm during the Great Depression, and Cesar had to assist them as they picked seasonal crops and lived in migrant villages.

Because of the family's constant relocations, young Chavez attended 67 different schools and never reached high school. He usually was not allowed to speak Spanish in school or on a school playground. In 1944 he joined the U.S. Navy. In his twenties, working for the Community Service Society in the *barrio* of San Jose, California, Chavez tried to improve living conditions. He helped 2,000 Mexican Americans register to vote.

In 1973 Chicanos proudly display their Aztlan flag.

Chavez moved his family to Delano, California, in 1963 and began a union. With his wife, Helen, and their children piled in a dilapidated car, he toured vineyards and visited 86 towns to organize Mexican American field-workers into his union.

He quickly ran out of funds, however, and had to ask for meals from his potential recruits. Chavez recalled:

> It turned out to be about the best thing I could have done, although at first it was hard on your pride. Some of our best members came that way. If people gave you their food, they'll give you their hearts.

Chavez's union began to grow. The first convention of the National Farm Workers' Association (NFWA), held in Fresno in 1963, brought together 287 delegates. The NFWA unfurled its own flag, an Aztec eagle in black on a white center surrounded by red. The members proudly called their union *La Causa*, or The Cause.

The union's first year was difficult. The $42 yearly dues proved so high for the 212 members that only 12 remained dues-paying members.

Chavez believed in Dr. King's philosophy of nonviolence. This caused some problems within his own family since Helen's father, Fabela, had served as a colonel in Pancho Villa's army during encounters with the Americans. Chavez remembered:

> Sometimes she [Helen] gets angry and tells me, "These scabs — you should deal with them sternly," and I kid her, "It must be too much of that Fabela blood in you."

Chavez carefully guided his NFWA away from the kind of violence that had long characterized relations between Mexican American laborers and their white bosses. He was stern and determined but also compassionate. Only once did he lose his temper and lash out, and that was when he and Helen went to a movie theater in Delano that segregated Chicanos, and he got into a fight.

In 1964 the NFWA, by emphasizing the Mexican American family and community needs, was able to increase its membership dramatically. The union had a thousand members. Most now paid their dues, and the union had $25,000 in its treasury. Chavez had not received a salary during 1963 and had to live off handouts, but in 1964 he was paid $40 a week. By making families the source of NFWA strength, he was able to recruit both women and men to his union. He also tried to avoid strikes, if he could.

From its position of strength within Chicano communities, Chavez's union first struck California vineyards in 1965 and began to win key concessions. He and other leaders were often jailed, but *La Causa* continued. The NFWA also began to receive backing from the kind of people who were also aiding Dr. King.

In the middle of the 1960s, Chavez launched nationwide boycotts of California grapes and lettuce to demonstrate that his seasonal laborers enjoyed strong outside backing across the nation. In 1965 when Filipino American grape pickers struck in Delano, the NFWA came to their aid. In 1966 Chavez's

Cesar Chavez (right) built a close relationship with the workers in his union.

union members began a 300-mile march to Sacramento to call attention to the grape strike. The union announced a national boycott of grapes:

> We have been farm workers for hundreds of years.… .
> Mexicans, Filipinos, Africans, and others, our ancestors
> were among those who founded this land and tamed its
> natural wilderness. But we…. are pioneers who blaze a
> trail out of the wilderness of hunger and deprivation that
> we have suffered even as our ancestors did.

In 1970, after the grape boycott had gone on for years, the largest corporations signed contracts with the union. In 1973 Chavez led his union into the AFL-CIO and changed its name to the United Farm Workers of America (UFWA). That year almost 5,000 men and women were arrested during efforts by growers to break UFWA strikes. When Nagi Daifullah, a young Arab American farm worker died after being clubbed by a strikebreaker, 10,000 Chicanos took part in the union's protest march. Juan de la Cruz, a 60-year-old Chicano, was shot to death two days later, and there was another protest parade.

Since he said his cause meant sacrifice, Chavez dramatized the plight of workers by fasting, once for 25 days. He also said,

> Fighting for social justice, it seems to me, is one of the
> profoundest ways in which man can say "yes" to man's
> dignity, and that really means sacrifice.

The growing political awareness of Mexican Americans found its way into other aspects of their lives. Many young people began to call themselves Chicanos, picking up a phrase that had originally been used to insult poor, landless Mexican American peasants. Now Chicano became a badge of pride. Some began to speak of La Raza, the race of people from which they came, to express their solidarity and pride. Ysidro Ramon Macia described Chicano characteristics as self-awareness and self-respect:

> He rejects the notion that he must subjugate his heritage
> in order to rise within American society. Instead, he
> presents the Anglo with the alternative to accept him as an
> equal. If the Anglo refuses to allow him his self-respect, as

is often the case, the Chicano now seeks to establish political and economic hegemony over his communities in order to control them and perpetuate his existence as a distinct entity.

Meanwhile, some Chicanos were gaining elective office. In 1964 Texas residents elected Henry B. Gonzales to the United States Congress, the first time in history the state was represented by a Mexican American. Gonzales criticized Chicanos who he felt had let their fury over racism lead them astray:

> I cannot accept the belief that simple, blind, and stupid hatred is an adequate response to simple, blind, and stupid hatred; I cannot accept the belief that playing at revolution produces anything beyond an excited imagination; and I cannot accept the belief that imitation leadership is a substitute for the real thing.

Other Chicanos also reached positions of political leadership. In 1974, Mexican-born Raul Castro was elected governor of Arizona. Ramona Acosta Baluelos, born in 1925, and a successful California businessman, was selected by President Richard Nixon in 1971 to be treasurer of the United States.

Chicano youths in Los Angeles staged school strikes in 1968 to demand respect for their culture and rights. Some students struck in Crystal City, Texas, and others in Denver, Colorado, where they carried signs reading "We Need a Chicano Principal; We Need Chicano Teachers." On college campuses from Minnesota to New Mexico, Chicanos demanded their own program of studies.

In 1969, 1,500 Chicanos met in the first Mexican American youth conference. Some Chicanos began to boycott segregated and inferior schools in Houston, Texas. In 1969 *La Raza Unida* (LRU) Party was begun to unite Mexican Americans because, as one leader said, "The two-party system is one animal with two heads eating out of the the same trough." LRU tried to influence or take over school boards and eliminate textbooks they considered racist.

In March 1974, Denver, Colorado, was the site of a unity rally attended by thousands of Chicanos, Puerto Ricans, Native Americans, and African Americans. It was addressed by Russell Means of the American Indian Movement. That August in

The Tijerina Raids

In 1966, in New Mexico, Reies Lopez Tijerina formed a society called the Federal Alliance of Land Grants. It sought to legally regain land taken from Chicanos since 1848. The Alliance stated,

Tijerina being taken to jail

> The Anglos should realize that the Spanish people of New Mexico... are uniting for the first time to recover and preserve their birthright and cultural heritage, and that each day they are getting stronger and more confident in themselves. The days of hopelessness for the Spanish people of New Mexico are numbered.

On June 5, 1967, Tijerina led his forces into the village of Tierra Amarilla, New Mexico, to protest land seizures by occupying the courthouse. Tijerina's supporters left voluntarily but mounted other protest raids. Tijerina himself was arrested on June 10.

The Alliance sought to join forces with Native Americans and African Americans, saying,

> For poor Chicanos and Indian people, the land is our mother — not private property. It is a means of survival, of production, that we both lost to the capitalist system and its values. ■

Albuquerque, New Mexico, Chicanos and Native Americans marched together in a "Solidarity Demonstration." This ethnic mixture united in another rally in Seattle, Washington, the next year.

Chicano women (or Chicanas) also began to meet and speak out against their "3-way oppression."

> Along with the racism and poverty suffered by all *Raza*, we endure oppression based on being a woman [sexism]. We see the need to change those so called "traditions" about women and to affirm the true tradition of strong, active Chicanas.

In 1975, 150 Chicano women struck against the Tolteca Foods plant in Richmond, California. Carrying signs saying "No Union, No Work, Sisters" and "The People United Will Never Be Defeated," they shut down the plant.

CHAPTER 8

THE RISE OF NATIVE AMERICANS

Young Native Americans, inspired by the civil rights and Black Power movements, sought to lift their people from depressed conditions. Indian life expectancy in the late '60s stood at 44 years compared to the national average of 64 years. For Native Americans, unemployment was more than double the national average, suicide three times the national average, and infant mortality four times the national average.

A young member of the AIM arrived in Washington, D.C., in 1972 to protest the role of the Bureau of Indian Affairs.

The American Indian Movement (AIM), founded in 1968 by Dennis Banks and others, promoted self-sufficiency for Native Americans, publicized the plight of Native Americans living on reservations, and tried to redress a host of grievances. The AIM's flag was an upside-down American flag, which Banks called, "the international distress signal for people in trouble." The AIM focused on reservation problems of cultural alienation, alcoholism, poverty, unemployment, and the weakening of Indian cultural bonds.

Dennis Banks came to the movement after years of failure as he tried to make something of himself. Born in 1932 in Minnesota to Chippewa parents, he was sent at age five to boarding schools far from home run by the Bureau of Indian Affairs. At these schools, he and other young Indians were forbidden to speak their native tongues and lost any knowledge of their ancient cultures.

Banks joined the United States Air Force and served in Japan but was unable to find a job when he returned to Minnesota. In 1966, when he and a white companion robbed a grocery store, his white accomplice was given probation, but Banks was sent to prison for two and a half years. He found that, while Native Americans constituted less than 7 percent of the South Dakota population, they made up about a quarter of the state's prison population. After Banks left prison, he began to organize the AIM.

On November 9, 1969, Banks and 78 Native American activists landed on Alcatraz Island in San Francisco Bay and took over the former federal prison there. They said they came to seize it as "Indian Territory." By the end of the month, nearly 600 Indians from 50 Indian nations camped on the island and claimed it "by right of discovery." When the U.S. government cut off telephones, electricity, and water, many left, but others remained.

Mocking the purchase of the island of Manhattan for $24 in the 1600s, the AIM offered to pay $24 for Alcatraz. In a seven-point paper, the AIM compared Alcatraz to federal Indian reservations:

1. It is isolated from modern facilities and without adequate means of transportation.
2. It has no fresh running water.
3. It has no adequate sanitation facilities.
4. There are no oil or mineral rights.
5. There is no industry, so unemployment is very great.
6. The soil is rocky and nonproductive, and the land does not support game.
7. There are no educational facilities.

The AIM announced its intention to make Alcatraz a center for Native American Studies, a spiritual center, an Indian Center of Ecology, a training school, and an American Indian Museum. Carol Williams, a Yurok Indian and mother of four children, said,

I have four children of my own. I want them to learn what the Indian people represented on this whole earth. What their heritage is — not just of their tribe, but of all tribes. We need more people. We need people with Indian ways to teach. We need people to teach languages, to tell what the different dances mean.

After 18 months, the occupiers were forcibly removed from Alcatraz.

But the AIM was just beginning its agitation. In February 1972, Russell Means, an Oglala Sioux and AIM leader, and 1,300 Indians in Gordon, Nebraska, protested the case of Raymond Yellow Thunder. At 51, this Oglala Sioux man was brutally beaten to death by two white brothers, and they were charged only with manslaughter rather than first-degree murder.

Seven months later, the Mohawk leader of the Alcatraz seizure, Richard Oakes, was slain. His white murderer also was tried for manslaughter, not murder (and was acquitted). Banks and other AIM leaders organized a Trail of Broken Treaties, a car caravan that headed toward Washington, D.C., to protest these injustices.

When they could not meet with top officials, as they had expected, a group marched into the Bureau of Indian Affairs. Riot police were called to remove the protesters from the building. When the police beat one Indian, the demonstrators seized the building and held it for five days. Their numbers increased to 500, and they renamed the building the Native American Embassy. Their action came just before the 1972 presidential election, and President Richard Nixon promised to appoint a committee to examine reservation life.

Protesters assemble at the Bureau of Indian Affairs in early November 1972.

The FBI investigated the AIM and later declared it "an extremist organization." Government funds for AIM schools were terminated.

In early 1973, the AIM's leaders, Dennis Banks and Russell Means, challenged federal power at a historic site, Wounded Knee, South Dakota. It was there in 1890 that 300 Sioux were massacred by the 7th Cavalry, effectively ending Indian armed resistance. Soon the AIM forces were surrounded by FBI agents and federal troops who cut off their food and other supplies. Gunfire was exchanged, for the Native Americans had come armed. Cease-fires were arranged and then broken. After 73 days, with casualties on both sides, the leaders of the AIM agreed to leave Wounded Knee on May 9, 1973.

Demonstrators in command of the Bureau of Indian Affairs building in late November 1972.

The U.S. Senate held hearings on major AIM complaints but made no changes in policy and corrected no problems. Instead, Banks and Means were arrested on ten felony counts for their part in the takeover. Their trial lasted for eight months in 1974. They were defended by Jewish American attorneys William Kunstler and

Mark Lane. At one point the judge ordered marshals to remove Kunstler, and another time he had Lane and Kunstler arrested for protesting too vigorously. Black entertainer Harry Belafonte helped raise funds for the defendants.

A government witness who said he saw Banks' and Means' supporters fire at FBI agents and marshals was proven to be a purjurer by his mother. When evidence was introduced showing that the FBI had altered documents and used illegal wiretaps and other unlawful methods to help build the prosecution's case, the judge dismissed all charges. Banks and Means in the meantime had lost eight months defending themselves.

By then, Banks was known as a highly respected voice of Native Americans. Often he was called on to mediate disputes between Native American nations and white government officials. Then, in 1975, a South Dakota jury found Banks guilty of rioting during a courthouse protest 18 months earlier. He refused to report for sentencing and fled with his wife to California. When he was arrested, Governor Jerry Brown ordered his release and refused to extradite him to South Dakota. California citizens, led by actors Marlon Brando and Jane Fonda, collected more than a million signatures on petitions backing the governor's actions.

Banks remained a free man as long as Brown was governor. He became chancellor of a Native American University in Davis, California, that adhered to Indian values and offered courses in health care, government, and financial planning. Banks left the state after Brown's term ended and in 1983 was granted asylum on the Onondaga Reservation near Syracuse, New York. There he coached a cross-country running club and organized clothing drives.

The next year, Banks agreed to return to South Dakota and was sentenced to three years in prison. Paroled in 1985, he returned to the Pine Ridge Reservation to "work at the local level." He persuaded the Honeywell Corporation to open a computer facility in Oglala, and other companies followed Honeywell's lead. The number of jobs on the reservation doubled.

On the reservation, Banks also was host of his own talk show on KILI, the only Indian-owned radio station. In 1990, Dennis Banks and Russell Means took part in a ceremony to commemorate the infamous cavalry massacre of Sioux at Wounded Knee.

CHAPTER 9

MULTICULTURAL AND BILINGUAL EDUCATION

The civil rights movement spurred a new interest in the African American legacy, a history that textbooks traditionally had omitted. By 1970, Black Studies programs and departments had been organized at Harvard, Yale, Columbia, and other universities, junior colleges, and high schools. Chicano students in California, New Mexico, and Texas also demanded courses that recognized their heritage. A Los Angeles high school student told a federal official:

> We look for others like ourselves in these history books,
> for something to be proud of being a Mexican, and all we
> see in books, magazines, films, and TV shows are
> stereotypes of a dark man with a tequila bottle in one
> hand, a dripping taco in the other... and a big sombrero.

In 1969 Dr. Rudolph Acuna began the first Chicano Studies department at the California State University at Northridge. In 1972 he wrote *Occupied in America: The Chicano's Struggle Toward Liberation*, the leading Chicano history textbook.

African American and Puerto Rican students in New York City united to campaign for courses about their people's contributions to the world. These successful protests soon brought additional requests for courses in the history of Italians, Scandinavians, Poles, and other white American ethnic groups. A new emphasis developed on multiethnic studies and the forgotten role of the many minorities who built America. Demands for Women's Studies also arose at this time as feminism became an increasingly powerful political force. Traditional educators and politicians scoffed that American society would be fragmented by this emphasis on different ethnic groups and by the denial that America was a "melting pot." Scholars increasingly had proven that the melting pot concept was either inaccurate or limited and that many people did not melt into a homogenized American culture. A new scholarship insisted America was really a "salad bowl" with distinct ingredients.

Spanish-speaking Americans voiced their pride in their cultural heritage and language. However, they had a major complaint about education in America. Their children attended a school system that taught all courses in English and was designed to promote the values of Anglo culture. School administrators, teachers, and guidance counselors devoted little time to the exploration of cultural or language differences, and school libraries did not have books in Spanish. Worse, many instructors had a disrespectful attitude toward students who did not speak English.

Few educators could speak Spanish (or any language other than English), and most showed no interest in the cultural heritages of people of color. The public school system in the United States had traditionally defined its role toward foreigners as that of Americanization and "assimilation." It sought to erase rather than preserve the language of recent arrivals from abroad.

This was a change from the days when vast numbers of immigrants from Europe reached these shores early in the century. Parochial schools in major cities had always preserved the religion, culture, and language of the homeland. And this approach often found its way into the public school system, especially when teachers were hired from the ranks of the immigrants.

Until the 1960s, Mexican Americans felt they had to accept an educational system that banned Spanish as a language and ignored their Mexican heritage. But after Dr. Martin Luther King, Jr., and Cesar Chavez spoke out, Chicanos began to challenge a school system that categorized their children as inferior because they did not know English. Many Chicano parents also reacted to the stress and humiliation the Anglo educational system imposed on their children. Chicano pupils dropped out of school after seven years, while white children averaged more than 12 years of education.

Educational and IQ tests based on English and middle-class cultural values posed a further threat to working-class Chicanos. Schools classified Chicano children as retarded two and a half times as often as other children. School administrators rarely hired bilingual teachers. Nor did they ask their staffs to shape curriculum or classroom procedures to the needs of their Chicano students.

No one disputed that Chicano children should learn English. But some teachers did more harm than good in the classroom by expressing contempt for Hispanic culture and the Spanish language and ridiculing children's accents and manners.

Chicano children who conformed to the demands of the school system found they had to reject the beliefs of their parents and the legacy of their ancestors. For this reason, schools, in the name of progress, generated conflict within Chicano families and communities. The unhappy result was that successful students often became outsiders among their own people.

The contest between the Anglo school and Chicano child continued without winners. The Chicano dropout rate remained high and educational progress low. Students faced the choice of rejecting either their education or their traditional culture and values.

Objective tests indicated that Chicano children had high aspirations, especially those from middle-class families. But in school they often were treated as lazy, slow, and unmotivated. Chicano students who should have seen education as an ally in the battle for success instead saw schools as a hostile force.

Responding to the demands of Spanish-speaking parents, Congress passed the Bilingual Education Act in 1968. But this was an issue that was not to be settled simply. Many people considered bilingualism bad educational policy and a dangerous political sop to the Spanish-speaking population.

Foes of bilingualism called it a wrongheaded, overly simple answer to a complicated problem. They claimed that it segregated Spanish-speaking children, hindered their learning of English, lowered their chances for economic success, and slowed their entrance into the American mainstream. Since bilingual classes were often geared for poor children and low achievers, middle-class parents who wanted "the best" for their children rejected them. The issue of bilingual education had not been resolved to the satisfaction of either side.

The Morgan School in Washington, D.C., in 1968.

CHAPTER 10

RIPPLES FROM THE SECOND AMERICAN REVOLUTION

The civil rights crusade has been called the Second American Revolution. Like the Revolution, it touched more than the people who fought its battles and reached beyond those who marched in its ranks. Dr. King and Malcolm X had an impact on more than new civil rights laws. These leaders stimulated a new pride and self-awareness among people of color and women.

In her history of American women, *Born for Liberty*, Sara Evans told how Dr. King's movement set the stage for feminism:

> The civil rights movement that grew from these activities provided a new model for social change and a language about equality, rights, and community that transformed public discourse in a decade. "Freedom now," the movement proclaimed.

African American pressure for equal rights helped win passage of the constitutional amendment that eliminated poll taxes. By requiring that citizens pay for voting, poll taxes had kept millions of poor white Southerners from exercising this privilege of citizenship.

After the Watts riot of 1965, Dr. King spoke with people from the neighborhood.

In 1990 the Americans with Disabilities Act swept through Congress. Senator Tom Harkin and other sponsors saw this law as part of the civil rights crusade, extending rights to disabled people who also faced many kinds of discrimination.

Beginning in 1964 at the University of California at Berkeley, student protests began to explode on college campuses. The Berkeley protest was sparked by demands for "free speech" after Berkeley's administration that summer had banned recruiters seeking students as volunteers for Mississippi's "Freedom Summer."

From a "free speech" fight, the campaign broadened its demands to include greater student rights, recruitment of people of color as professors, and initiation of multicultural courses. Over the next six years, protesting college students often adopted nonviolent techniques developed by African Americans in the South.

By this time, students, often led by people of color, became the backbone of the antiwar movement that swept the country. Antiwar protesters sang "We Shall Overcome" and talked of Black Power, Brown Power, and People Power.

Michael Harrington's War

President John F. Kennedy died in Dallas in 1963 before he could announce his "War on Poverty." President Lyndon Johnson announced it the next year. But it was a war that had already been declared in 1962 by Irish American socialist Michael Harrington. His book, *The Other America*, explored the long-standing and cross-cultural nature of rural and urban poverty in the world's richest democracy. Harrington piled up dry statistics and gritty, unpleasant truths. True to his deeply held Catholic socialist beliefs, Harrington was profoundly moved by the civil rights crusade.

Johnson's war was much more brief than the one envisioned by Harrington. Federal officials arrived in urban ghettos and hired a few token residents to help run their programs. Millions of dollars were spent, and most of it went for "overhead." All the federal funds for Harlem added up to only $25 per resident.

The war on poverty had hardly been launched when President Johnson changed his priorities. He poured enormous amounts of men, firepower, and money into the war in Vietnam and had few resources left for the war against poverty. "The war on poverty," said Dr. King, "died on the battlefields of Vietnam." ∎

Reies Tijerina (left), Native American spokesman Al Bridges (center), and Ralph Abernathy (right), leader of the Poor People's March on Washington

In 1968, protest activities escalated. In early April Dr. King had been trying to help striking garbage collectors in Memphis, Tennessee, win a strike. He also had thrown himself into the antiwar movement, and he had been planning a huge, nonviolent Poor People's March on the nation's capital that would unite African Americans, Native Americans, Mexican Americans, Puerto Ricans, and poor whites from Appalachia and the cities of America.

Dr. King returned to Memphis and told a church meeting he was not afraid to face his fate. "I may not get to the mountaintop with you," he told his listeners, but he predicted that his people would get there. The next evening, while standing on the balcony outside his motel room, King was assassinated.

Within hours of the murder, 172 urban ghettoes erupted in violence. Furious people took to the streets to loot and destroy. By the time King's body was carried on a simple mule cart to its final resting place, 32 people had died, 3,500 had been injured, and 27,000 had been arrested. President Johnson ordered 4,000 troops to Baltimore, 5,000 to Chicago, and 11,000 to Washington, D.C. It was an unfit ending for a life dedicated to nonviolence.

The funeral of Dr. Martin Luther King was simple and moving.

A fatherless Poor People's March limped into Washington. A Resurrection City of tents spread out near the Lincoln Memorial to house the multiethnic marchers. Leaders of the American Indian Movement, the civil rights movement, and the Chicano movement tried to breath strength into the tent colony. But heavy spring rains reduced grassy streets and tent floors to thick mud. Congress ignored the hopes of Resurrection City's residents, and city police finally forced the protesters to pack up and leave.

Though King had died in violence, his crusading effort continued to generate resistance and hope for people of color. Native Americans were inspired by his example to demand justice. In 1969 Chicano leader Reies Tijerina, founder and director of the Alliance of Free City-States, was jailed when he challenged Anglo seizures of Mexican land in New Mexico and demanded the government show "good faith to the Indo-Hispano" people. From his cell, he wrote a "Letter from the Santa Fe Jail" which was inspired by Dr. King's famous "Letter from a Birmingham Jail." Tijerina said, "Like the black people, we too have been criminally ignored."

Chicano leader Rudolfo "Corky" Gonzales was influenced by Dr. King and the Black Power movement. In 1969 he said,

> We can understand that we are a nation of *Aztlan*. We can understand and identify with Puerto Rican liberation. We can understand and identify with black liberation. We can understand and identify with white liberation from this oppressing system once we organize around ourselves.

In 1976, the Chicano Communications Center of Albuquerque, New Mexico, reached the same conclusions that characterized Dr. King's opposition to the Vietnam War:

> The eyes of our people are opening wide. We no longer see only a small part of the picture. We see that our *barrios* are all over the world, and the whole world is our *barrio*....

> In the early 1960s, great numbers of black people began fighting the same enemies as ours. Whites began to oppose the Vietnam War. And we also began to move again.

> Our struggle broke out on three fronts at once: In New Mexico, it was for the land — *la tierra*. In California, it was for the right of farm workers to unionize. In many places it was for the right to live free of racist discrimination and abuse — especially from the police and school system. As in the black movement and later the Native American [movement], we saw a high tide of nationalism: "I'm proud to be Chicano!"... It was a response to generations of racism. *Con estos gritos* (with these slogans), our minds were liberated from years of brainwashing, not knowing our own history and culture, hating ourselves, wanting to be white. We asserted our peoplehood, our *Raza*, with joy and pride. New Chicano art, theater, and newspapers flowered to put across the new message.

In 1968 and 1969 this poster, showing the Mexican revolutionary Emiliano Zapata, was displayed in many New Mexican villages. The poster reads "Land or Death."

The movement inspired by Dr. King and Malcolm X stimulated pride among American citizens who had been taught to be ashamed of or to hide their race, ethnicity, or color. Black children learned that "Black is Beautiful" and that their ancestors had had a history in Africa and in the New World. Other people of color made similar discoveries.

Ethnic awareness began to blossom in America in the late 1960s. It was expressed first by lapel buttons such as "Polish is Beautiful," "Kiss Me, I'm Italian," and "I'm Puerto Rican and Proud."

In 1989 students organized a prodemocracy protest in Beijing's Tiananmen Square and sang "We Shall Overcome." They were inspired by Dr. King's nonviolent resistance to tyranny in America.

In New York City's Harlem, National Memorial African Bookstore owner Louis Michaux (right) displays a photo of Malcolm X.

CHAPTER 11

THURGOOD MARSHALL

Wielding the law as his weapon, Thurgood Marshall became known as "Mr. Civil Rights" and was the first African American to sit on the United States Supreme Court. When he appointed Marshall to the high court in 1967, President Lyndon Johnson said, "Thurgood Marshall symbolizes what is best about our American society — the belief that human rights must be satisfied through the orderly process of law." Few disagreed.

Marshall was born in 1908 in Baltimore, Maryland. His mother was a teacher, and his father was a waiter. Both knew their people's history and eagerly passed their knowledge on to their children.

Marshall's parents taught him to think for himself, to study hard, and to defend his principles. His father, Marshall recalled, taught him to argue by challenging his own logic and making him prove what he said. It was good training for what was to come.

At first young Thurgood was a poor pupil more interested in mischief than research. His school principal regularly punished him by sending him to the school basement to memorize sections of the Constitution. Marshall left elementary school with low grades and a thorough knowledge of the Constitution.

Still full of fun, in 1925 Marshall enrolled in Lincoln University in Oxford, Pennsylvania, hoping to become a dentist. By then, he was 200 pounds, over six feet in height, and athletic. One night he and five of his classmates drove into Oxford for a movie. Marshall refused to sit in the balcony that was reserved for people of color and led his friends to front-row seats on the main floor. They waved off an usher who told them to obey the rules. An angry white had some nasty words for Marshall. "You can't really tell what that kind of person looks like," Marshall later recalled, "because it's just an ugly feeling that's looking at you, not a real face." He responded that he paid for his ticket and would sit where ever he wanted. At that moment the movie theater's segregation policy ended.

As an attorney, Marshall had a long and distinguished career arguing cases for the NAACP.

At Lincoln University, Marshall learned about such heroic figures as W.E.B. Du Bois and Paul Robeson and began to discover his own identity. He also met Vivian Burey at a church dance, and they fell in love. By the time they married in September 1929, he had decided to become an attorney. Marshall graduated with honors from Lincoln the following June.

Marshall applied to the University of Maryland Law School, but it had never had an African American and turned him down. He was accepted at Howard University, the nation's leading black higher-education institution. There he met and was inspired by Professor Charles Houston, one of the first African American graduates of Harvard Law School. A demanding and dedicated teacher, Houston made Howard's law school one of the best in the country.

In 1933 Marshall graduated from Howard University a top student in his law class. In the midst of the Great Depression, he found few clients with the cash to pay their legal fees, but he persevered. The next year Houston was appointed chief of the new legal arm of the NAACP, and he sent for Marshall.

In New York City the two men worked on discrimination cases around the country — winning a few and losing others — each time hoping they could end a bit of segregation in American life. In 1938 Houston left his post at the NAACP, and Marshall, who was then 30 years old, became chief of the NAACP legal department (renamed the NAACP Legal Defense Fund in 1940).

Marshall and his wife lived in a small, walk-up apartment in Harlem. He worked long hours and traveled 5,000 miles a year seeking out cases and building support in African American communities. He defended black men who had been beaten by the police until they confessed to crimes they had not committed. He marched on picket lines to protest the use of child labor and to demand higher wages and shorter hours for steelworkers.

In 1946 he defended Herman Sweatt who had been accepted at the University of Texas Law School but was told to sit in the hallway outside of classes attended by whites. About 200 white Texan students had collected enough money to hire an NAACP lawyer for Sweatt. Marshall submitted his brief against those submitted by 11 southern state legal departments. For the first time, however, the Justice Department supported the NAACP claim that racial segregation was unconstitutional. Five years later the Supreme Court ruled that Sweatt must receive equal treatment.

Marshall then prepared to overturn the infamous *Plessy* case of 1896 that had declared segregation the law of the land. African American parents had challenged school segregation in Kansas and in four southern states. Just for bringing forth these cases, some parents had lost their jobs, and families had suffered.

The NAACP sought to prove in the foremost of these cases, *Brown v. Topeka Board of Education*, that racial separation harmed black children. Marshall called on Dr. Kenneth Clark to testify. Born to parents of African descent in the Panama Canal Zone in 1914, Clark had received his doctorate at Columbia University in 1940 and had become a leading psychologist. He had used black dolls and white dolls to study the impact of segregation on children. From the groups of dolls, Dr. Clark had asked African American children to choose the doll they thought was nice, the one that looked bad, the one that had a nice color, the one that was their favorite, and the one "most like you."

Most African American children in segregated schools invariably picked white dolls as their favorites and said the white dolls had a nice color. The children usually said the black doll was bad. Most disheartening for Clark was that half of the African American children said the doll most like them was the white doll. The tests results were virtually the same for children from ages 3 to 9 years.

Marshall had argued 15 cases before the Supreme Court and only lost two, but this case was the crucial one. His opposing counsel was John Davis, 81, an attorney who had argued 250 cases before the high court and had once turned down a chance to sit on the Supreme Court. The two men argued for three tense days.

Nine months later Chief Justice Fred Vinson died and was replaced by Earl Warren, a former governor of California. During World War II, Warren had urged placing Japanese Americans in internment camps. How would he and the court now see segregation?

The Warren Court asked for additional arguments from Davis and Marshall. In May 1954, Chief Justice Warren read the high court's unanimous decision. It read: Segregation in education was unconstitutional.

Marshall and his NAACP team were elated. White segregationists in the South were not. School desegregation began in the upper South and the North, but violent resistance exploded wherever desegregation was attempted in the Deep South.

In 1956 Marshall (right) represented Autherine Lucy (center) for the NAACP. Roy Wilkins, director of the NAACP, is at left.

Marshall was busy during the civil rights era fighting other famous cases. Autherine Lucy was turned away by the University of Alabama law school even though a federal judge had ruled she was qualified to attend the school and had ordered her admission. Though Marshall carried the *Lucy* case to the Supreme Court and won, the university banned Lucy anyway "for her own safety."

Marshall argued for an end to bus segregation in Montgomery, Alabama, when Dr. King and his followers boycotted the buses. In Little Rock, Arkansas, he entered the case when Governor Orval Faubus fought the federal government's decision to send troops to enforce desegregation. The NAACP supported the sit-ins in southern lunch counters, and Marshall argued these cases.

He was now traveling 50,000 miles a year and handling more than 500 cases involving upward of 2,000 people. He turned down an offer of a $50,000-a-year job because his NAACP work was too important to leave.

In 1961, President John F. Kennedy appointed Marshall a federal judge. After some hesitation, Marshall took the appointment. In four years he wrote 100 opinions, and not one of his decisions was reversed by the Supreme Court.

In 1965, Marshall accepted an appointment as solicitor general of the United States. As the third legal officer behind the attorney general, it was Marshall who could decide which cases the federal government would appeal to the Supreme Court. He won many cases against the Ku Klux Klan and for enforcement of civil rights.

On June 13, 1967, President Johnson appointed Marshall an associate justice of the U. S. Supreme Court, saying, "I believe it is the right thing to do, the right time to do it, the right man, and the right place." The fight against discrimination was picking up steam, and the new justice struck blows for liberty from his new position. When the court turned increasingly conservative after Johnson's term ended, Marshall became known for his dissenting opinions. In 1978, in the *Bakke* case, he pointed out a simple truth:

> The experience of Negroes in America has been different in kind, not just in degree, from that of other ethnic groups. It is not merely the history of slavery alone but also that a whole people were marked as inferior by law.... The dream of America as the great melting pot has not been realized for the Negro; because of his skin color he never even made it into the pot....

Marshall continued to dissent, and others listened. Sandra Day O'Connor, the first woman to sit on the high court, recalled Marshall's contribution to discussions among the justices:

> At oral arguments and conference meetings, in opinions and dissents, Justice Marshall imparted not only his legal acumen but also his life experiences, pushing and prodding us to respond not only to the persuasiveness of legal argument but also to the power of moral truth.

In 1991, Marshall, citing poor health, retired from the Supreme Court, but he continued to speak out on public issues until his death in 1993. Considered one of the greatest liberal voices and one of the finest legal minds of the century, he had advanced the cause of equality in the United States.

Supreme Court Justice Thurgood Marshall (far left) with other Supreme Court Justices.

CHAPTER 12

THE POLICY OF "BENIGN NEGLECT"

During the Newark riots of 1967, ghetto residents confront National Guard troops.

In the summer of 1964, America's ghettoes began to explode in violence. Rioting first struck Harlem then broke out that summer in Brooklyn and Rochester, New York, and in Jersey City and Paterson, New Jersey. The circumstances might be different, but the overall pattern was the same. Disturbances usually were triggered by charges of police brutality during the arrest of ghetto residents. Mostly young black males took to the streets to mark their rage. Sometimes women joined in, and some whites also participated.

The rioting was not affected by Congress' passage of civil rights acts in 1964 and 1965. These laws focused on discrimination in southern states but did little for the deteriorating urban ghettoes.

Ghetto riots were often a desperate response to poverty and hopelessness. Ghetto residents did not own their own homes or manage their own neighborhoods. Few were hired to work in the white-owned stores in their neighborhoods. Public schools did not prepare the young for decent jobs or college, and white teachers often insulted the children and ignored their heritage. Ghetto social services were few and inadequate. Garbage collection was haphazard. Perhaps most aggravating to residents, the white police force behaved like a foreign army in occupied territory.

In 1965 in Atlanta, this family lived in poverty but hoped voting rights would improve their lot.

Riots also erupted in the Puerto Rican *barrios* of Chicago in June 1966; Perth Amboy, New Jersey, in August 1966;

Paterson, New Jersey, in July 1968; Trenton, New Jersey, in June 1969; Passaic, New Jersey, in August 1969; and in Jersey City, New Jersey, in June 1970. But the largest riot took place in 1965 in Watts, the largely African American neighborhood of Los Angeles, California. Watts' unemployment rate was three times the white national average. Watts did not even have a public transportation system to take its residents to jobs.

The National Guard had to bring in armored vehicles during the Newark riots in 1967.

Following an instance of police brutality, Watts exploded with shouts of "Burn, Baby, Burn," as rioters destroyed entire blocks. When the smoke cleared, 34 were dead, more than a thousand were injured, and some 4,000 people had been arrested.

In 1967, rioting reached 164 cities, leaving 82 dead, 3,400 injured, and 18,800 arrested. Full-scale revolts shook Newark, which had 23 deaths and Detroit, which had 43. Again and again residents' rage was directed at white police and white stores. However, many African American homes and businesses also went up in flames. And almost all the casualties were people of color.

President Johnson appointed a commission headed by Illinois governor Otto Kerner to investigate the causes of the riots. The commission found that the root cause of the ghetto problems was "white racism." The disturbances stemmed from years of bitterness over poverty, chronic joblessness, police brutality, inadequate homes and schools, and government neglect of these massive problems. Ghettoes, the commission found, were owned by outsiders who drained the wealth from these communities and then rode home to the suburbs.

The Kerner Commission urged immediate governmental and private programs to rebuild decaying and now burned-out inner cities. Ghetto dwellers, the report said, had every right to govern themselves and control their economic life. It issued this warning: "Our nation is moving toward two societies, one black, one white — separate and unequal."

Never before had a government study pointed out the role of white Americans in creating ghetto conditions. Never had a government commission painted so bleak a picture of the nation's future. President Johnson did not endorse the report and did not act on its findings. A year later the Kerner Commission reported that the trend toward two societies had continued.

President Johnson and then President Richard Nixon chose to adopt another document by scholar and politician Daniel Patrick Moynihan called *The Negro Family: The Case for National Action*, which shifted the blame for ghetto problems away from a white society that owned and ran black economic life. Instead, Moynihan's report located the source of ghetto trouble in the absence of fathers and the "pathology" of the "matriarchal" African American family.

This reasoning ignored the survival strategies of poor black women, which rested on an elastic family structure that included kin and close friends who were often considered relatives. Blacks created large networks of "family" that shared meager welfare checks and other resources to take care of the young and the aged. For example, because of this network's effectiveness, very few black children have been put up for adoption.

Rules imposed by local welfare systems also insured that many husbands in poor areas would float in and out of their families. Unemployment, underemployment, and low wages also limited the home role for fathers. But women remained the primary shepherds of the family network. Aiding black families was a powerful African American church system, which served as a port in every kind of emotional or economic storm.

This student demonstration at Howard University was one of hundreds to rock college campuses in 1968.

Middle-class whites, often competitive and individualistic, had little understanding of the value of these cooperative family networks in poor African American communities. Moynihan's report urged "benign neglect" in treating ghetto problems. By "benign neglect" he meant ghetto problems should be ignored by the federal government.

The United States was also divided and in turmoil over the Vietnam War during the late 1960s. In the first six months of 1968, 221 major demonstrations had taken place on 101 college campuses. In early March a political unknown, Senator Eugene McCarthy, won 42 percent of the vote in the Democratic presidential primary in New Hampshire against President Johnson. By the end of March, Johnson said he would not seek another term in the White House.

Four days later Dr. Martin Luther King, Jr., was assassinated in Memphis, Tennessee, and a hundred cities exploded in violence. In early June, after Robert F. Kennedy won the crucial California Democratic presidential primary, he, too, was assassinated.

The Democratic convention that August was marked by violence. Chicago police repeatedly charged into antiwar demonstrators outside the convention hall. Inside, party leaders desperately tried to heal their wounds and unite behind their presidential candidate, Hubert Humphrey. The Republicans nominated Richard Nixon, and were able to capitalize on the popular slogan of "law and order," a backlash against the antiwar and student demonstrations and the exploding ghettoes.

In 1968 Nixon ran against a Democratic Party divided against itself. He blamed ghetto rioting on the Democrats and said the War on Poverty had incited people to riot by raising unrealistic expectations. Nixon skillfully played on middle-class fears that rioting might spread to white residential areas.

The blacklash had also opened the way for another "law and order" presidential hopeful. Segregationist George Wallace, running as an independent, told audiences the majority of white Americans were being treated with neglect and hostility by the government, the political parties, and the courts. Wallace received 9,446,167 votes, or 13 percent of the total votes cast. Never before had a candidate openly proclaiming racist ideas received so large a vote.

Nixon defeated Humphrey by less than a million votes. During his administration, he reduced aid for cities, welfare, day-care and drug rehabilitation centers, job training, and other social programs associated with the Democrats and the War on Poverty.

The Nixon administration adopted the policy of "benign neglect" toward ghetto problems. Major cities continued to deteriorate, and some riot areas of the 1960s were never rebuilt. Nixon did allocate funds for his program called "Black Capitalism," but no African American was invited to serve in the Nixon cabinet.

Civil rights organizations warned that neglect of the ghettoes was "like ignoring cancer." Repeatedly and in vain, African American leaders requested aid for those who could not find jobs, develop skills, or take care of themselves. But a new era, strongly dominated by a backlash, had begun.

CHAPTER 13

OPENING THE POLITICAL PROCESS

Dr. King's focus on the right to vote changed American politics. U.S. government officials before 1963 had almost all been white, Anglo-Saxon, and male. Only a handful were women or people of color. For example, in 1964 the entire country had only 280 elected African American officials in mostly minor offices.

The profound changes brought to the South by the civil rights crusade and the laws it sparked had little impact on the North. People in northern ghettoes could vote but had no reason to, since they were offered few acceptable candidates. Black districts had been gerrymandered, or manipulated, to insure the election of white candidates. For example, the huge Brooklyn neighborhood of Bedford Stuyvesant, populated mostly by African Americans, had not been able to elect a Black to Congress until 1968.

African Americans in the North were not held back by restrictive signs or laws but by customs and bigoted attitudes. In Connecticut, a white businessman boasted to a group of his friends, "I got a colored boy from Harvard working for me, and he's holding down a white man's job." Most African American men did not even have a chance for any kind of "white man's job." Even the federal officials who ran the War on Poverty in ghetto neighborhoods rarely hired more than a few token Blacks in top positions.

In 1965, however, President Johnson began to select African Americans for high posts in the federal government. He appointed Thurgood Marshall solicitor general of the United States and Hobart Taylor as a director of the Export-Import Bank. Patricia Harris became the first African American woman to serve as an American ambassador.

Blacks in cities were also advancing on their own. J. Raymond Jones became the head of Tammany Hall in New York City.

Constance Baker Motley was elected borough president of Manhattan, the highest elective post ever held by an African American woman.

Robert Weaver (left) was sworn in by Justice Arthur Goldberg (front right).

In 1966 Floyd McCree became mayor of Flint, Michigan, and Robert Henry became mayor of Springfield, Ohio. Edward Brooke, a Republican, was elected to the United States Senate from Massachusetts, a state with a 3 percent black population. He was the first African American U.S. senator in almost a hundred years.

That year President Johnson appointed Robert Weaver as his secretary of housing and urban development. Weaver became the first African American to serve in a presidential cabinet. He had been part of President Franklin Roosevelt's "Black Brain Trust." Johnson also appointed Andrew Brimmer to the Federal Reserve Board and Constance Baker Motley to a federal judgeship.

Activist Julian Bond at the 1968 Democratic convention.

In 1967 new victories marked Mississippi elections when a black candidate won the first seat in the state's legislature in the 20th century. A total of 21 other Blacks won county or local posts in the state.

In 1967 African Americans also gained nationally. The Supreme Court ruled that states could no longer ban interracial marriages, overturning centuries of legal intervention into people's private choices. Black mayors were elected in two large cities — Gary, Indiana, and Cleveland, Ohio. And also that year air force major Robert Lawrence was chosen to serve as an astronaut.

By 1968, there were eight African American members of Congress, 11 federal judges, and seven ambassadors. The Democratic National Convention in 1968 had 212 black delegates. Julian Bond's name was placed in nomination for vice president, but he declined , saying that, at age 28, he was too young.

Also in 1968 there were 79 state representatives, 18 state senators, and seven mayors of cities who were African Americans. In all, 1,702 African Americans held elective or appointive offices on state, county, and local levels. In 1968 Shirley Chisholm, a Brooklyn teacher, became the first African American woman elected to Congress. By 1970, 1,469 African Americans held elective office.

Andrew Young served as an aide to Dr. King, congressman from Georgia, U.S. delegate to the UN, and mayor of Atlanta.

In 1972 Andrew Young of Georgia, an assistant to Dr. King, and Barbara Jordan of Texas were both elected to the Congress. They were the first African Americans to represent southern states in Congress since Reconstruction.

Shirley Chisholm, Congresswoman

Born in 1924 in Brooklyn, New York, to poor parents, Shirley Chisholm was destined to set some records. After serving four years in the New York State Legislature, in 1968 she became the first African American woman elected to Congress and four years later became the first African American woman to enter the presidential race.

Chisholm graduated from Brooklyn College in 1946 and spent many years working in day-care centers and as the director of her own nursery school. In later life she earned many awards for her contributions to early childhood education.

Calling herself "unbought and unbossed," Chisholm continued to represent her Bedford-Stuyvesant district in Congress until her retirement in 1983. Her familiarity with Spanish helped her reach her district's large Spanish-speaking population. Chisholm defined her priorities.

> Our children, our jobless men, our deprived, rejected, and starving fellow citizens must come first. For this reason, I intend to vote "No" on every money bill that comes to the floor of this House that provides any funds for the Department of Defense.

Chisholm became an outspoken opponent of the Vietnam War. She also championed efforts to provide aid for Native Americans, Chicanos, Hispanic migrant workers, African Americans, and women.

When Chisholm announced her presidential candidacy in January 1972, she was not taken very seriously by the media. She, however, called herself a serious contender and "the candidate of the people." She raised issues the other candidates chose to ignore. In 1973, she wrote *The Good Fight* to describe her presidential campaign.

Chisholm won many awards for her service to human rights, to children, and to her community. She once said,

> We Americans have a chance to become someday a nation in which all racial stocks and classes can exist in their own selfhoods but meet on a basis of respect and equality and live together, socially, economically, and politically.... I hope I did a little to make it happen. I am going to keep trying to make it happen as long as I am able. ∎

Congresswoman Shirley Chisholm opened her campaign for the presidency in Boston in 1972.

Barbara Jordan

Barbara Jordan, who was destined for great things, was born poor in Houston, Texas in 1936. Jordan's grandfather, who made a living collecting junk, told her repeatedly that she was a special person. He smiled when he said, "I've seen a lot, and I can tell."

Jordan attended segregated classes in Texas although she soon began to wonder why segregation had to be. Later she decided she wanted to become an attorney. In 1959 she graduated from Boston University Law School and then returned to Texas as a lawyer. Since she could not afford to open an office at the time, she saw her clients in her parent's dining room.

In 1960, Jordan worked to elect Senator John F. Kennedy president. She began by stuffing envelopes in an office and finished by giving speeches to cheering audiences. People liked her commanding speaking voice and urged her to run for office. Twice she ran for the Texas State Senate and lost, but in 1966 she finally won.

In 1972, Jordan was elected to the House of Representatives, becoming the first African American to represent Texas in Congress. She played an important role in the debates leading to the vote to impeach President Nixon.

Jordan was elected to Congress two more times. In 1976 at the Democratic National Convention, she delivered the keynote speech, the first time this honor was given to an African American. She worked hard to get Democrat Jimmy Carter elected to the White House.

In 1979 Barbara Jordan retired from Congress and became a professor at the University of Texas. In 1992 she again made an appearance on nationwide television as a speaker at the Democratic National Convention. In her stirring speech, she said that this country should revive its concern for the unfortunate and the persecuted, and she denounced all forms of racism as wrongheaded and divisive for America. ■

The number of African Americans in Congress by 1985 reached 20, and the number of black mayors in cities rose to 286. Blacks had been elected to city halls in Detroit, Michigan; Gary, Indiana; Washington, D.C.; Atlanta, Georgia; and New Orleans, Louisiana. In Fayette, Mississippi, Charles Evers, brother of the murdered civil rights leader Medgar Evers, was elected mayor. Tom Bradley, elected mayor of Los Angeles in 1973, was elected four more times until in 1992, he decided to retire at age 72. In 1983 Harold Washington

Charles Evers

In 1964 Puerto Rican Americans staged a silent protest outside of New York's City Hall against segregation in schools.

formed a unique coalition of African American, Catholic, and Jewish voters to win election as a reform mayor of Chicago. He was reelected in 1987 and died in office in 1989.

The voting rights law of 1965 also immediately boosted Puerto Rican political participation. The new law abolished literacy tests in English for the Spanish-speaking populace and permitted people who had achieved a sixth-grade education in a school where English was not the primary language to vote. Many citizens who could not speak English but who had been educated in Puerto Rico could now vote or hold office.

In 1968, four Puerto Ricans were elected to the New York legislature. Robert Garcia went to the state senate and Armando Montano, Luis Nine, and Manuel Ramos were elected to the assembly. That same year Joseph Monserrat was chosen to serve on the New York City Board of Education.

In 1969, Herman Badillo was elected to Congress from the Bronx, becoming the first Puerto Rican to win this high post. He went on to serve as borough president of the Bronx and to run for mayor of New York City. His success paved the way for the election of other Puerto Ricans to high city offices. When Robert Garcia was elected to Congress from the Bronx in 1978, he became the first New York-born Puerto Rican to serve in Congress.

The civil rights movement and the voting rights law widened political opportunities for Mexican Americans as well. In 1965, New Mexicans elected Joseph Montoya to the United States Senate. The next year Eligio de la Garza won election to Congress in Texas, and Manuel Luzan, Jr., was sent to Congress from New Mexico.

These victories opened avenues for other qualified Mexican Americans. In 1971, Samuel Zachary Montoya was appointed a justice of the New Mexico Supreme Court. The next year Raul Castro was elected the first Mexican American governor of Arizona.

In 1974, Jerry Apodaca was elected New Mexico's first Hispanic governor since 1918, and in 1977, President Jimmy Carter picked Lionel Castillo to become his commissioner of immigration and naturalization.

Asian Americans also continued their climb in American politics. In 1962 Korean American Alfred Song was elected to the California State Assembly and then reelected by a landslide. In 1966 William Soo Hoo, a Chinese American, was elected mayor of Oxnard, California. What made his election unusual was that Oxnard had only 60 other Chinese American citizens among its 64,000 residents.

In 1964 Arab American George Kasem represented California in the United States House of Representatives.

Beginning in 1964, Arab Americans, too, began to win high elective offices. That year George Kasem became the first Arab American elected to the House of Representatives. Abraham Kazen, Jr., the son of a Lebanese immigrant, was elected to Congress from Texas, in 1966, and he was reelected eight times.

Arab Americans also won seats in other parts of the country. For example, James Deeb was elected to the Florida State Senate. In 1970 William Nahas was elected mayor of New London, Connecticut. The next year Sabah Najor became Michigan's secretary of state. James Tayoun was elected to the Pennsylvania State Legislature in 1969 and again in 1973 and 1975. In 1975 Anthony Abraham was elected to the Florida State Legislature. The next year Herb Macol was elected mayor of Mankato, Minnesota. Nick Robert Rahall was elected to Congress from West Virginia in 1976 and many times after that.

As congressman, senator, and private citizen, Arab American James Abourezk enjoyed a distinguished career.

James Abourezk had a long and distinguished career in public office. His father had migrated from Lebanon in 1895 and had become a peddler. James was born on the Rosebud Sioux Indian Reservation in South Dakota. In 1970, he was elected to Congress. Elected to the Senate in 1974, Abourezk served until 1979 when he decided to leave for private legal practice. As an attorney, he spoke for the rights of Palestinians and Native Americans and tried to correct the stereotypes of Arabs depicted in the American media. His South Dakota successor to the Senate was another Arab American, James Abdour, who served from 1981 to 1987.

In 1974 Arab American Edward Hanna was elected mayor of Utica, New York, a city with a tiny Arab American community.

Ted Weiss

Born in the Hungarian village of Gava in 1927, Ted Weiss fled with his family in the 1930s to escape anti-Semitism. In the United States, young Ted mastered English in six months. In 1946 he joined the army and served in Japan. Weiss graduated from law school and became an assistant district attorney in New York City. In 1960 he was elected to the New York City Council where he wrote a gun-control law and served for 14 years.

In 1976 voters in a multiethnic district of Manhattan sent Weiss to the U.S. House of Representatives. He served in Congress for the next 17 years, earning a reputation as an unswerving liberal in the tradition of Franklin Roosevelt and John Kennedy, fighting for equal rights, civil liberties, poverty programs for the poor, and money for AIDS research. He said the Reagan and Bush administrations had handed the country to the rich and betrayed the poor and people of color.

Weiss was not afraid to stand alone. Once he was the only one in Congress to vote against a law he felt imperiled civil liberties. When President Reagan ordered the invasion of Grenada in 1983, Weiss said the invasion was illegal and called for the president's impeachment. Former New York City mayor Edward Koch said of Ted Weiss:

> There were times I thought he would impeach God, but the fact is, even then you knew he would be intellectually honest. You knew he thought God should be impeached.

In 1992 Weiss entered the New York City Democratic primary election race once again seeking his party's nomination to run for Congress. Weiss died just before the primary election but still won a majority of the votes in his district. He had lived his life in service and with commitment. ■

Hanna took only $1 of his $20,000 salary and also ran five of the city's departments to demonstrate his public dedication. He removed his office doors to make himself more available to the city's citizens.

In 1975 George Latimer, a Lebanese American, was elected mayor of St. Paul, Minnesota, and then reelected five times. In Oregon, Victor Atiyeh served as governor from 1979 to 1987.

Lebanese American John Sununu, a three-term governor of New Hampshire, became President Bush's first White House chief of staff. In this post he became the most powerful force behind the president.

CHAPTER 14

REOPENING THE IMMIGRANTS' DOOR

Although Presidents Truman, Eisenhower, and Kennedy called on Congress to end the discriminatory immigration laws of the 1920s, nothing happened. The United States quota system still discriminated against people from Asia, Africa, the West Indies, and eastern and southern Europe and favored people from northern Europe. Not until 1965 under Lyndon Johnson's administration was a new era started in immigration history.

Standing in the shadow of the Statue of Liberty, President Johnson signed the new law that eliminated all previous quotas based on religion or nationality. The law had another laudable goal — family reunion — since the old law had kept many immigrant families divided.

Nevertheless, Congress did not open the door to all who wanted to enter. Americans, according to polls, opposed unrestricted immigration by a two-to-one majority. So Congress imposed a ceiling on immigration of 290,000 a year. Of these, 120,000 would come from the Western Hemisphere and 170,000 from the Eastern Hemisphere. No ceilings limited people by country, race, or religion, and refugees could enter under special categories.

Many immigrants became American citizens during a special ceremony at Ellis Island in September 1990.

Since the new law recognized that previous acts and practices had prevented many foreigners from being united with their American families, immediate family members of those already living here were given 74 percent of the available visas. Immigrants with professional status who had long been excluded for reasons of race and ethnicity also began to enter America from underdeveloped countries.

The pattern of immigration to America changed dramatically after 1965. Between 1920 and 1960, Europeans made up 60 percent of all immigrants, South and Central Americans 35 percent, and Asians 3 percent. Between 1965 and 1974, arrivals from North America, Central America, and the West Indies fell from 43 percent to 38 percent, from South America from 10 percent to 5 percent, and from Europe from 38 percent to 21 percent. Those from Asia rose from 7 percent to 34 percent. Percentages for Africa and Oceania remained the same, though the numbers had doubled. In 1975 Europeans accounted for 19 percent of immigrants, South and Central Americans 43 percent, and Asians 34 percent.

Open Letter to Armenian Immigrants

In 1976 Reverend G. H. Chopourian, a prominent Armenian American, welcomed newcomers from abroad with this letter.

Welcome to the United States, land of liberty and mother of opportunity! Our communities greet you and extend a warm hand of fellowship....

There was a time when, in some parts of this country, an Armenian was not accepted to be a witness at court, was excluded from certain organizations and clubs, and was considered to be a third-class citizen. By hard labor, by strong ambition, by purposeful cooperation Armenians achieved an enviable standard and made a name for themselves as hardworking, honest, industrious, intelligent, and wholesomely ambitious people....

They were among the early settlers in America and as immigrants did everything possible to preserve their culture and to adjust to American ways. They went to school, learned trades, engaged in commerce, built churches and schools, formed associations, published papers, and created today's rather dynamic Armenian American community. This is a remarkable achievement. They want to preserve this record and want your cooperation....

The Armenian American community is happy to have you here and willing to help in every way possible. It is only by unified efforts that we can achieve our goals. Come to us if you need guidance. Keeping our own standards high, it is important to accept American standards, benefit from the vast possibilities that the United States offers without misusing them. Speak Armenian, but learn how to speak English, too. ■

For those ethnic groups that had tiny quotas for decades, the changes were enormous. Portugal sent 300 immigrants in 1965 and 11,000 a decade later. In the next 10 years, Portuguese immigrants soared to 30,000. Greeks, originally restricted to 308 entrants yearly, made 8,917 visa applications in the first year of the new law. Between 1966 and 1975, 129,000 Greeks arrived here.

Arab nations had sent only 2,000 people over several decades, but between 1968 and 1970, some 37,600 Arabs arrived. After the new law was enacted, 15,000 Koreans arrived each year, many fleeing the tensions of war and dictatorial rule. By 1986, 30,000 Koreans arrived yearly, and Korean Americans numbered almost a million.

Chinese immigrants, previously limited to 105 people a year, sent over 17,508 during the new law's first year. An additional 9,770 Chinese here on a temporary basis became permanent legal residents. By 1967, Chinese arrivals were up to 25,000 a year, most of whom were males. Of the 115,509 who landed here in the five years after 1965, however, women and men came in equal numbers.

In 1965 India sent 300 immigrants to America, and in ten years the figure rose to 14,000. Filipino immigrants, held to 105 entrants before the 1965 law, numbered more than 25,000 in 1973 alone.

Settlement patterns of ethnic groups also changed. In 1969, 50 percent of the Mexican immigrants, 13 percent of the Canadians, 39 percent of the Filipinos, 36 percent of the Chinese, and 20 percent of the Portuguese chose to settle in California. New York was the choice of 44 percent of the Italian immigrants, 36 percent of the Poles, 25 percent of the Chinese, and 18 percent of the Cubans. Most arrivals still wanted to live near their American relatives and close to industrial centers where they could find employment.

In the Southwest, another migration pattern continued. Many Mexicans crossed and recrossed the U.S. border as illegal aliens. In the 1970s four million immigrants legally entered the United States, and an estimated eight million came illegally. Most of the latter were Mexicans crossing a common border with the United States. In 1970 the Immigration and Naturalization Service (INS) captured 145,000 illegal Mexican migrants, or about 80 percent of all illegal entries. Most of those seized were employed young men seeking better-paying jobs in the United States and supporting more than three others in Mexico. By 1980, the illegal entry figure was estimated at half a million, most of them Mexican farm workers.

In the 1970s millions of Mexicans legally entered the United States at the Texas border, but more arrived illegally.

COMBATING ARAB STEREOTYPES

Beginning with the birth of the state of Israel in 1948, turmoil and occasional warfare flared in the Middle East, and many Arab people left for the United States. However, they arrived in a country with a Middle Eastern policy based on an alliance with Israel, the major recipient of U.S. foreign aid. America's State Department viewed Arab nations as undemocratic, warlike, and untrustworthy, and the media often cast individual Arabs in hostile stereotypes.

In 1973, when this photo was taken, Arab Americans had begun to demonstrate against U.S. policy in the Middle East.

To aid their families in the Middle East and challenge media stereotypes in the United States, Arab immigrants began to form their own American societies. In 1975 the American Lebanese League in Washington, D.C., was concerned with the turmoil and death in Lebanon and sought to publicize issues from a Maronite Christian viewpoint. The Lebanon Information Center, also in Washington, D.C., represented major Christian political societies interested in Lebanon.

The American media since 1948 had portrayed the violence between Israelis and Palestinians in simplistic terms as a fight between good and evil. But this began to change with more balanced news from Israel coupled with Palestinian American efforts to articulate their viewpoint. In 1979 the first African American United States ambassador to the United Nations, Andrew Young, secretly opened talks with the Palestine Liberation Organization (PLO). The talks were unauthorized, and U.S. policy opposed any contacts with the PLO, which had been labeled "a terrorist organization." Major American Jewish groups demanded that President Carter remove Young, and the president did. However, Arab Americans saw Young as a pioneer peacemaker for bringing the PLO into the deadlocked negotiations between Israel and the Palestinians. Young finally resigned.

As brutal warfare tore Lebanon apart in the 1980s, American organizations sought to care for innocent families caught up in the war. The organization Save Lebanon was founded in 1981 to provide medical aid for victims of the fighting, especially children. It also published constructive proposals for ending the warfare. In 1983, the American Druze Public Affairs Committee was founded to publicize Muslim Druze participation in Lebanon.

In 1980, the Arab American Anti-Discrimination Committee, under former senator James Abourezk, was formed with branches across the country to combat media distortions of the image of Arab people and the prejudice Arab Americans faced in their communities. The committee said it enrolled citizens "from all walks of life" and aimed to give Arab Americans "a united voice on issues that concern us." It "strongly objected to the negative stereotypes against Arabs which pervade the American media" and pledged itself to fight all discrimination against Arabs. It also publicized the contributions Arab Americans made to "America's melting pot."

Other groups have followed. The Arab American Institute, founded in 1985, encouraged people to vote and run for public office. The next year the Lebanese Americans in Fresno, California, collected enough money to bring 16 teenagers from war-torn Lebanon to America for a six-week summer free of conflict. The teenagers were placed with families, each family receiving a pair, a Druze Christian and a Muslim youth, so the students could return to their homeland with experience in reconciliation.

The turmoil and death in Lebanon drove many refugees here. But unlike poor Europeans who arrived at the turn of the century, the Arab newcomers were more often intellectuals, students, and the highly educated. Shi'ites, one of the main branches of the Muslim faith, also began to arrive and seek jobs in cities such as Detroit. Their new life was not without its pains. Many were torn between abandoning a war-torn homeland that needed their brain power and settling in a peaceful country that welcomed and rewarded their skills.

Ralph Nader

Ralph Nader was born in 1934 to a Lebanese immigrant father who owned a bakery and restaurant in Connecticut. He attended Princeton University on a scholarship, studied hard, and graduated at the top of his class. At Harvard Law School, Nader gained a reputation for leading a life free of smoking, drinking, parties, and fun. He attended few movies and plays and had few dates. He became engrossed with car injury cases and wrote an article, "American Cars: Designed for Death." Young Nader had grasped a cause that would become his career — protection of the human body from man-made perils.

After graduating from Harvard, Nader practiced law, and as a specialist in car safety, worked for Senators Daniel Moynihan and Abraham Ribicoff. In 1965 Nader wrote *Unsafe at Any Speed: The Designed-in Dangers of the American Automobile*, which became a bestseller and made Nader a celebrity. His book leveled serious charges — that General Motors had produced a dangerous car in the Corvair and that General Motors executives knew this and refused to do anything about it for four years.

Nader was just beginning. After the young crusader testified before Ribicoff's Senate committee on the lack of car safety, General Motors hired agents to shadow him and try to wreck his career. One agent admitted in court that he had tried "to get something" on Nader to "shut him up." Nader sued GM for $26 million and collected $280,000. In 1966 the Congress passed a car safety law that was a tribute to the diligent work of Ralph Nader.

Nader took his book royalties and any money he earned and poured the cash into further research. He extended his campaign to protect consumers from car manufacturers and meat packers, and from unsafe trucks and paper mills that polluted the environment. He investigated banks and supermarkets that cheated the public. One critic charged, "He is just plain against consumption."

Nader was soon able to establish "Nader's Raiders," a group of young attorneys dedicated to defending the consumer. They labored in cramped quarters and were paid little for their long hours of hard work. Nader had no secretary and poured his $200,000 a year salary into his crusade, spending only $5,000 yearly on himself. An unpaid spy network inside the corporations he investigated supplied Nader's Raiders with facts and details about business frauds and harmful products.

Ralph Nader still fights a dogged uphill battle against the most powerful forces in America, and he does not often win. But this is a fight he feels he owes his fellow citizens. ■

C H A P T E R   16

A MAJORITY
SEEKS EQUALITY

In 1964 as the civil rights bill was brought to the floor for a vote in Congress, Representative Howard Smith, 81, believed he had a fool-proof strategy to insure its defeat. He appended a provision called Title VII that extended the act's benefits to women. He reasoned that liberals would oppose the provision because it might defeat the entire bill. He believed that Title VII would cause the rest of Congress to "laugh the bill to death."

By suddenly broadening the bill's coverage, Smith thought he would divide its supporters, strengthen its foes, and arouse new opposition. The maneuver failed and the most far-reaching civil rights law in a century sailed through Congress. People of color and women together took a giant step toward equality.

This advance by the two groups had deep historical roots. American women first realized their oppression and learned to fight for their rights while opposing slavery. The first women's rights convention in Seneca Falls, New York, in 1848, grew out of the experiences of women as crusading abolitionists.

Many women began to rethink their lives in 1963. That year Betty Friedan's study, *The Feminine Mystique*, pictured women as unfulfilled souls trapped in housework and tied down by society's rules. Friedan said that women, especially the educated and highly motivated, did not have to settle for that if they wanted better. That same year the report of the Presidential Commission on the Status of Women forced men and women to reexamine women's place in society. Then came the civil rights struggles in the South, in which women played a major role. Women watched in shock as police used dogs and fire hoses against women, men, and children. Finally, the new civil rights law, and its Title VII, placed equality for women alongside equality for people of color.

Betty Friedan wrote The Feminine Mystique *in 1963 and three years later became a founder of the National Organization for Women (NOW).*

Society's traditional roles for women came under sharp attack in 1964 during Mississippi's "Freedom Summer." Women volunteer civil rights workers found Mississippi in 1964 was a wake-up call. While supporting the African American drive for justice, these women learned about their own oppression. Male leaders invited them to type, run copy machines, teach school, address letters, cook, and clean. They were assigned the many "housekeeping" tasks of the crusade. But when men met to set policy and plan strategy, women were not invited to take part. That work, they were told, was man's work.

Yet all around them were brave, resourceful African American women — Rosa Parks, Ella Baker, Fannie Lou Hamer, Coretta Scott King. It did not take highly educated, confident, and competent young white women too much time to rebel.

A small group of women began to meet and complain about their limited role in the SNCC. One, Ruby Doris Smith, presented a paper, "The Position of Women in SNCC," based on these sessions. SNCC chairman Stokely Carmichael and other men greeted her paper with a shrug.

Far from discouraged, the women who took part in the Freedom Summer continued to meet, talk, and plan. In the fight for liberty, they said, women should not have to forego their own freedom. They insisted that men who fought for racial justice should understand that women deserved no less.

In 1965, Casey Hayden and Mary King of the SNCC wrote a paper that denounced the assignment of female civil rights workers to minor roles and male domination. Many men scorned their protests, but a few listened.

Women in the 1960s also began to counter their lowly status in revolutionary student groups. They began to demand the floor in meetings of the radical Students for a Democratic Society (SDS). In 1968, Beverly Jones and Judith Brown wrote a book to denounce the "desperate attempt of [SDS] men to defend their power by refusing to participate in open public discussion with women."

> You are allowed [in SDS] to participate and to speak, only the men stopped listening when you do. How many times have you seen a women enter the discussion only to have it resume at the exact point from which she made her

departure, as though she had never said anything at all? How many times have you seen men get up and actually walk out of a room while a woman speaks, or begin to whisper to each other as she starts?

Women who raised such questions were called names, and they were accused of hating men and undermining progress. At an SDS convention, those who called for discussion of women's liberation were hit with tomatoes and escorted out of the hall. Women in draft resistance groups were told men had to be the leaders.

Though many women still remained in these groups, they often formed caucuses to discuss their problems and push their own agenda. Others decided that, in order to define their identities, they should leave the groups and mount campaigns free of male interference. In organizations where freedom and justice were at stake, women insisted they would no longer be taken for granted or hide their own drive for equality.

Entering Nontraditional Professions

The women's movement had a dramatic impact on the number of women entering nontraditional professions. The number of women attending law schools rose from 4,715 in 1969 to 16,760 in 1973. The number of women in medical schools rose from 3,392 to 7,825 in the same period. The number of women carpenters, electricians, and auto mechanics doubled. The number of women engineers in 1960 was 7,000 and rose to 19,600 by 1973.

The women's movement also had an impact on elementary education. Many more men became willing to enter a field society had reserved for women. There were 140,000 male elementary school teachers in 1960 and 231,000 in 1970. ■

The 1960s were years of great change for women. The decade began with 17 women, the highest number in history, sitting in the Congress; two in the Senate and 15 in the House of Representatives.

Title VII suddenly placed discrimination based on sex in the same illegal category as acts of hate based on color, race, religion, or national origin. By the end of 1964, 24 states had established commissions on "the Status of Women." In 1967, all the states had them.

At first women's liberation was not taken seriously. Comedians relied on "women's lib" jokes for their biggest laughs. If Title VII was enforced, some people joked, a Playboy Club might have to hire male "bunnies."

Women also faced grim, entrenched political foes who relied on established traditions. An "old boy's network" that thrived on mocking women also had no intention of making space for women executives in business or government. As late as 1973, Secretary of State Henry Kissinger was quoted as saying, "For me, women are only amusing, a hobby. No one spends too much time on a hobby." Such attitudes were uttered by cabinet members and cabdrivers, foremen and factory workers, local sheriffs and waiters. Many women also held similar attitudes.

The women's movement, however, increased its pace in 1966 when Betty Friedan and 27 other women founded the National Organization of Women (NOW), the first outspoken feminist society since the 19th century. "We chipped in $5.00 [each], began to discuss names [for our group]. I dreamed up NOW on the spur of the moment," recalled Friedan.

NOW's founding statement said,

It is no longer either necessary or possible for women to devote the greater part of their lives to child-rearing.

Some of NOW's first members came from the ranks of those who had stood by the side of the SNCC, CORE, SCLC, and the NAACP in the South. These women had learned that equality required new laws, which then had to be followed by public pressure. NOW demanded hearings on the enforcement provisions of Title VII.

NOW leaders were skilled lobbyists, but they were weak at organization, and they let the United Auto Workers Union handle their mailings. NOW hoped for good responses to their letters but were disappointed. In 1967, NOW called for a women's Bill of Rights that included an Equal Rights Amendment (ERA) to the Constitution, as well as laws banning sex discrimination. NOW also asked for child-care centers for working women, tax deductions for working parents who had home and child-care expenses, equal educational opportunity, maternity leave benefits, and women's right to control their bodies, including the right to legal abortions.

NOW pickets marched in front of the *New York Times* to protest "help wanted" ads that separated jobs for men from those for women. President Johnson soon signed Executive Order No. 11375

"Battling Bella"

Bella Savitsky was born in 1920 in the Bronx, New York City, to Russian Jewish immigrants. She attended public schools and went to Hunter College because it was free. She attended Columbia Law School on a scholarship and graduated in 1947 at the top of her class. She married Martin Abzug, and they had two daughters.

As an attorney, Mrs. Abzug took cases others refused to handle. She appeared in a Mississippi court in 1951 to try to stop the state from executing an African American accused of a rape he had not committed. She lost the case, but continued to fight for justice for people of color. She also dared to defend men and women accused of communism during the McCarthy Red scare era.

In the 1960s Abzug helped write bills that became part of the Civil Rights Act of 1964 and the Voting Rights Act of 1965. She was active in peace movements and became a founder of the Women's Strike for Peace. Abzug also supported liberal members of the Democratic Party.

In 1971, when she was elected to Congress from Manhattan, Abzug became the first Jewish American congresswoman in history. On her first day at the Capitol, she introduced a resolution calling for the withdrawal of U.S. troops in Southeast Asia. She tried to abolish the military draft, and she took part in public hearings on American war crimes in Vietnam. By then she was called "Battling Bella" and was well known for her sensationally large hats.

Abzug became a leading member of NOW and a founding member of the National Women's Political Caucus. Elected twice more to Congress, she sponsored the Freedom of Information Act that allowed citizens to read any files kept about them by the FBI or CIA. In 1976 Abzug decided to run for the Senate and lost. She ran for mayor of New York City the next year and lost that race, too. The following year she lost another bid for Congress.

But Abzug's career was not finished. She lectured and wrote columns and a book about how women could gain political power. She explained one of her great aims:

> What I try to do is make women feel that there isn't anything they can't do if they want to. And when I speak to them or meet with them, I try to give them that feeling, that this is their right. ■

Women demonstrated for equal job and educational rights.

that prohibited sex discrimination in federal employment or by anyone doing business with the government.

Conservative groups, such as Business and Professional Women's Clubs (BPW) and its 170,000 members, joined campaigns against both subtle and open discrimination toward women. In late 1967, NOW began to pressure the Equal Employment Opportunity Commission (EEOC) to enforce Title VII. NOW pickets marched before EEOC offices during a National Day of Demonstration. In early 1968, NOW sued EEOC to force it to comply with its own rules.

More radical feminist groups formed. Their demands went far beyond the economic issues of job security and advancement. Some women began to demand that abortion become a basic right of privacy for all women. "If men could become pregnant, abortion would be made legal, cheap, and available in no time," said one feminist.

In 1968, 200 women staged a protest at the Miss America Pageant in Atlantic City, New Jersey. They used the traditional beauty contest to declare that women were more than attractive bodies to be paraded before men. Demonstrators threatened to burn "oppressive" clothing, such as bras and high-heeled shoes. Nothing was burned though. Nevertheless, the media ridiculed the "bra-burners" in an effort to make fun of a serious movement that dared to oppose ancient male-imposed rules.

In 1968, the year of uprisings by students, African Americans, Chicanos, and others, the revolt of feminists did not go unnoticed. That November over 200 women from 37 states and Canada convened in Chicago for the first women's liberation conference. Weeks later the Human Rights for Women, Inc., formed as the first women's legal defense group, pledged to fight sex discrimination.

In 1969, President Richard Nixon appointed Elizabeth Koontz to head the Women's Bureau of the federal government, but for the first time since 1932, no woman sat in a presidential cabinet. Congresswoman Florence Dwyer sent a letter to President Nixon that assailed his administration for doing "nothing of significance" for women and for replacing many women officials with men.

CHAPTER 17

"SISTERHOOD IS POWERFUL"

In 1970, women constituted only 5 percent of the nation's state legislators and less than half a percent of the country's urban mayors. Though only two percent of the Congress of the United States were women, 52 percent of the United States population was female. In four states — Arizona, Louisiana, Nevada, and New Mexico — husbands legally controlled the family wealth, including their wives' wages. In every state a woman's legal residence was where her husband lived, and in Alabama, Florida, North Carolina, and Texas, women could not sell their property without their husband's consent. Yet women had been voting for 50 years.

These restrictions in the land of the free led women, under the slogan "Sisterhood Is Powerful," to step up their drive for equality. Feminism moved in new directions as it picked up steam. Women wanted to examine how and why society continued to carry out dominant male views of women. In middle-class urban and suburban areas women's "consciousness-raising" sessions met in homes and community centers to discuss how society affected their own views of themselves. They discussed personal feelings, their status, the kinds of resistance they faced in life, and the meaning and destiny of their lives. Sessions ranged far afield, discussing women at home and as wives, mothers, and daughters.

Women began to conclude that men functioned in a public world, while women ruled and made decisions in the private domain. As women examined the private sphere of American life they had been assigned, they found it was "political."

The personal, some women began to say, was political. Sara Ruddick was a graduate of Harvard trying to write her doctoral thesis. Her participation in the feminist movement "enabled me to achieve a new self-respect at home, made me confident and clear about my need for the friendship of women." She discovered that her ambitions and interests beyond the home had weighed her down when they "should have been a source of pride." This happened, she reasoned, because she — like most women — accepted society's evaluation of her proper role.

Feminist scholars found that women's societies had changed American life for the better and that women had been prominent reformers when governments refused to play a reform role. They discovered that even women who stayed at home with their children and family performed deeply political functions.

Radical women's groups used phrases such as "male chauvinism" or "male supremacy" to describe attitudes that denied women freedom. Colleges began to offer Women's Studies courses. Radio stations began to devote more time to news about women. Educational institutions examined their hiring practices to eliminate "sexism" or discrimination against women on faculty and in classes.

Feminism picked up converts and provoked resentment. A familiar charge was that feminists had gone too far. They undermined family life and values. They burned bras in public, made life miserable for their husbands or boyfriends, and defamed true womanhood with their outrageous behavior.

Was it eccentric for women to picket the New York City Marriage License Bureau to protest that marriage was demeaning and oppressive to women? Many women and men thought so. But more men and women than before thought they had a point. Was it outlandish for a female junior high school pupil to sue in order to take a sheet metal course or to play on a softball team? Was it absurd for women to demand positions in the fire, police, and other city departments traditionally reserved for men? Or were all of these demands simply a matter of citizens' rights?

As the debate swirled on, women found more than their voices. They discovered the techniques that gained civil rights for minorities could be used by them. During Senate hearings on the constitutional amendment to enfranchise 18-year-olds, 21 women from NOW disrupted the proceedings to demand the Senate schedule hearings on the proposed Equal Rights Amendment.

The United Auto Workers Union in 1970 became the first union to endorse the Equal Rights Amendment. A week later Senate hearings were held on the ERA. Five weeks later Representative Martha Griffiths forced the ERA out of the House Judiciary Committee and onto the floor of Congress. Two days later the Women's Bureau of the Department of Labor reversed its earlier stance and announced it would support ERA.

Meanwhile, women's groups began to challenge the very concept of "man's work." In June 1970, NOW filed a legal complaint that sex discrimination was being commonly practiced by 1,300 major American corporations. A month later, the Justice Department filed its first complaint under Title VII of the Civil Rights Act. To celebrate the 50th anniversary of passage of the women's suffrage amendment, women in major cities held demonstrations for equality of the sexes. They had three demands:

1. Equal opportunity in employment and education.
2. Free abortion on demand.
3. 24-hour child-care centers.

By this time, women marched on many fronts. They demanded a greater role in church hierarchies, including official ordination as

Feminism and Race

Women of color experienced a double oppression in America for being part of both the "wrong" sex and the "wrong" race. However, feminism attracted few women of color in its early years.

The reasons for this were understandable. White feminists were usually middle class or upper class, and were looking for a "different family structure." African American women, on the other hand, were trying to stabilize their families. They often felt that racial oppression was overwhelming compared to male domination, and to raise questions of sexism was divisive.

However, Congressperson Shirley Chisholm told an audience:

[The] harshest discrimination that I have encountered in the political arena is antifeminism both from males and brainwashed, Uncle Tom females. When I first announced that I was running for the United States Congress, both males and females advised me, as they had when I ran for the New York State Legislature, to go back to teaching — a woman's vocation — and leave politics to the men. ■

ministers. Catholic women asked their church to allow them to be priests but to no avail. Jewish women began to study to become rabbis.

Women no longer wanted to be underpaid stewardesses on planes while men designated as bursars did the same work and received higher wages. Women wanted to be cast in movies and TV dramas as strong, intelligent, and independent rather than stereotyped as weak and fearful, needing men to complete their lives. They wanted to be doctors as well as nurses, pilots as well as den mothers, basketball players as well as cheerleaders.

Feminists argued for a vocabulary that used not "mankind" but "humankind," not "policeman" but "police," not "chairman" but "chair," not "congressman" but "congressperson."

In 1978 a parade for the ERA had in its front line (from left to right) Bella Abzug, Gloria Steinem, and Betty Friedan.

To many men, some women were stirring a dangerous tempest in a family teapot. Some women wanted to keep their own names after marriage. Women wanted to learn carpentry, plumbing, and electronics. Some wanted to be pages in Congress, bat girls for baseball teams, and firefighters. Others said their husbands or boyfriends had to help wash the dishes, clean the house, and take care of the children, and all wanted something done about rape. They pointed out that rape was not a sexual act but a terrible example of a man's wish to hurt and humiliate a woman.

Some women sought a more directly political role. In the summer of 1971, over 200 met in Washington to form the National Women's Political Caucus (NWPC). Its founders included congressional representatives Bella Abzug and Shirley Chisholm and authors Betty Friedan and Gloria Steinem. Many of the women present had taken part in student rebellions, the civil rights movement, or the antiwar movement. More than a few had been arrested for their activism on behalf of peace and women. Now they mobilized to fight as women underrepresented in government posts.

By the school fall term in 1971, the first course in women's history was taught at Stoughton High School in Wisconsin. Over a hundred newspapers, journals, and newsletters reported on women's issues, reflecting a new feminism in the United States. Students in high schools and colleges began to learn that history

Boys Will Be Boys

In the spring of 1973 Debra Dulberg and Laurie Lehman, sophomores at Clark University, wanted to play competitive tennis doubles, but their college had no women's team. They persuaded Coach Ed Trachtenberg they deserved a place on Clark's junior varsity, a men's team. The pair went off to play a match against Worcester Junior College.

The Dulberg-Lehman doubles team decisively defeated their male opponents. The coach of the losing team sent his version of the match to the Worcester, Massachusetts, *Telegram and Gazette*. The published account of the match stated that Clark University's David Dulberg and Larry Lehman had been victorious.

Coach Trachtenberg called the losing coach about the mistake. The losing coach called back days later to explain that his men had been "so embarrassed" about "losing to girls." The paper agreed to print a small item that identified the victors as Debra Dulberg and Laurie Lehman.

Both of these women later earned doctoral degrees in the field of psychology. They also continued to play competitive tennis against both men and women. ■

was not made just by white men in business suits sitting in board-rooms or in government offices. They learned that women of all colors had fought in wars, petitioned for peace, helped win the vote, and promoted equality and justice for minorities and themselves.

Feminists and their many male supporters rejoiced in 1972 when the Equal Rights Amendment was approved in the Senate and in the House of Representatives and sent to the states for ratification. Within months it was ratified by 20 states and seemed on its way to victory. Many male-dominated groups, including unions of teachers and teamsters, announced support for the amendment. In June 1982 the Equal Rights Amendment was finally defeated when it fell three states short of ratification.

In 1972 Congress passed and President Nixon signed an Education Act that included Title IX which prohibited discrimination in all educational programs that received federal aid. From early childhood to college levels, the new law began to bring a revolution not only in the hiring and promoting of teachers, but in the many aspects of American society that education touched. Schools had to open noncontact sports to girls as well as boys. Females had a right to play softball, tennis, and basketball in officially recognized school leagues. Female students could join boys in sheet metal, electrical, and woodworking classes.

Even before this law was passed, young minority women had brought test cases to court in New York City. Alice de Rivera in 1969 won the right to attend all-male Stuyvesant High School. Bonnie Cruz Sanchez sued in court for her right to take a metalwork shop class in her high school. In 1970 she passed the course and won the school's top metalwork prize. Sanchez was helped in her quest by her mother, who had also been denied the right to take a school metalwork course twenty years earlier.

The response of men to the demands of women varied. Some were confused, others were angry, and a few were happy about surrendering their privileged position. However, most men still wanted an exemption from housework, shopping, and cooking. Role reversal was hardly easy.

Justice Sandra Day O'Connor

Until 1981, no woman had ever sat on the United States Supreme Court. Then there was Sandra Day O'Connor. Some Americans considered it ironic that the first woman to serve on the Supreme Court was nominated by President Ronald Reagan, a man who showed little interest in the women's movement. But O'Connor was Reagan's choice for the first opening on the high court.

Born in Texas in 1930, Sandra Day received a law degree in 1952 and soon after married a classmate from law school. The couple settled in Phoenix, Arizona, practiced law, and raised three children. In the 1960s, Mrs. O'Connor entered Republican Party politics. She advanced rapidly from assistant attorney general to state senator to Senate majority leader to superior court judge. Along the way, Justice O'Connor gained a reputation for being a tough, methodical, and fair jurist.

President Reagan was pleased with his choice for the high court. Here was a candidate of the right gender and conservative outlook he sought. On the court, Justice O'Connor immediately distinguished herself as a thoughtful jurist who was hard to label. Her appointment to the Supreme Court has earned her a place in history. ∎

CHAPTER 18

MARCHING INTO THE 1980S

Americans greeted the Bicentennial of the Revolution of 1776 happy for something to celebrate. The state of the republic in the years immediately preceding the Bicentennial had not been heartening. For the first time a vice president, Spiro Agnew, had resigned after being charged with fraud committed when he had been governor of Maryland, and Representative Gerald Ford had been picked by President Nixon to complete Agnew's term.

Americans then watched the long, sordid saga of Watergate unfold on TV and in the press. A president and his chief aides had ordered political "dirty" tricks, illegal break-ins, an unauthorized invasion of Cambodia, and then carried out a massive, illegal cover-up.

Watergate ended with the resignation of President Nixon who was pardoned by incoming President Ford. Many citizens believed the Nixon pardon had halted the wheels of justice, but Ford felt the pardon helped heal the country's wounds after Watergate.

In 1976, the Democratic governor of Georgia, Jimmy Carter, defeated Ford to win the White House. Carter had won only 45 percent of the white southern vote, but black southern voters helped make the white Georgian president. African Americans had come to trust this man who called himself a "born-again Christian" and admitted he had not opposed racism until late in life. They even forgave Carter when, early in his election campaign, he publicly said he favored "ethnic purity" in neighborhoods.

In office, President Carter appointed more African Americans to high positions than any previous president. He picked Patricia Harris as his secretary of housing and urban development. She became the first

In 1965 Patricia Harris became the first African American woman ambassador for the United States.

Judge John Sirica

In 1904 in Connecticut, John J. Sirica was born to a mother who ran a grocery store and a father who had immigrated from Naples in 1887 and became a barber. John remembered how the family waged "an uphill fight against poverty." He sold newspapers, became a waiter, and at age 17 enrolled in law school. He quit to take up boxing, won one ten-round fight, quit, and went back to graduate from law school in 1926.

John Sirica dabbled in Republican politics, worked for the U.S. attorney general, and then began a private law practice. President Dwight D. Eisenhower appointed him a federal judge in Washington, D.C., in the 1950s.

In 1972 Judge Sirica was the presiding judge when the Watergate burglars were brought to his court. He knew the men were hiding something and said he "did not want to be party to a whitewash." Judge Sirica pressed the defendants so relentlessly they began to admit their orders came from higher up. In time, Sirica presided over the trial of President Nixon's chief aides. He also ordered that a grand jury report on the president be sent to the House Impeachment Committee. For two years Sirica demanded that the truth be told about Watergate. Sirica said,

I would hope frankly — not only as a judge but as a citizen of a great country and one of millions of Americans who are looking for certain answers — I would hope that the Senate is granted power by Congress by a broad enough resolution to get to the bottom of what happened in this case.

U.S. District Court Judge Sirica twice ordered President Nixon to turn over secret tapes made at the White House. When Nixon took the issue to the Supreme Court, the Court agreed with Sirica. If Judge Sirica had not pursued the truth as strongly as he did, the revelations of Watergate might never have unfolded for everyone to see. Sirica died at age 88 in 1992. ∎

African American woman to sit in a presidential cabinet. Carter and Harris journeyed to the depressed South Bronx to meet with New York City's Abraham Beame, the city's first Jewish American mayor, to plan urban renewal programs.

Carter named nine African Americans as ambassadors to African and Caribbean nations and to such countries as East Germany, Spain, and Romania. The president set a record in opening the White House to African American delegations.

President Carter felt it was important to change the Federal Court of Appeals, which had become a bastion of white male power. This court heard 40,000 appeals cases, while the Supreme Court heard only about 100. No woman had served on the appeals court. President Eisenhower appointed no Blacks to the court of appeals, Kennedy appointed one, Lyndon Johnson appointed two, and Richard Nixon and Gerald Ford appointed none.

By contrast, Jimmy Carter appointed nine African Americans to the court of appeals, including the first African American woman, Amalya L. Kearse, and 21 other African Americans to lower federal district courts. In four years Carter appointed more African American federal judges than Presidents Nixon, Ford, Kennedy, and Johnson combined.

Carter's appointments and programs did not improve the basic conditions of the poor. The jobless rate for people of color was double the rate for whites, and 31 percent of African Americans lived below the poverty line. Carter also began budget cuts in social welfare programs that would be continued by Republican administrations.

A growing African American middle class had found places as doctors, dentists, professors, models, historians, salespeople, public officials, and architects. Black millionaires owned publishing, banking, and insurance companies. Once denied the chance to play in professional sports, black figures almost dominated baseball diamonds, basketball courts, and football fields. Along with famous entertainers, some joined a growing class of African American millionaires.

African Americans who held top positions in major corporations owed their progress to the sacrifices of civil rights activists. They benefited from "affirmative action" programs initiated in the 1960s. These required employers to consider nonwhite applicants for every position. Some employers, however, tried to avoid compliance with affirmative action programs. And some African American beneficiaries did not acknowledge their debt to the civil rights crusade. Appreciated or not, the doors had been pushed open, and people of color had prospered in a system that once was rigged against them.

President Carter also had to deal with thousand of refugees from Caribbean dictatorships. Hundreds left Haiti on small crafts, only to be turned back by federal immigration officials who ruled

This elderly Cuban refugee is being helped ashore by a U.S. marine in Key West, Florida.

they were not really political refugees but were seeking economic advancement. The question of Haitian refugees continued for the next two decades and often divided policymakers.

In April 1980, thousands of Cubans left by boat from Cuba to Florida. Some 1,500 federal officials were rushed to Florida to process the Cubans' entry into the United States as anticommunist refugees. About 400 were detained because they were mentally or physically ill, or because they were criminals. The welcome given the Cubans, who were largely white, was often contrasted with the rejection that greeted most Haitians, who were usually black. By the end of 1980, 125,000 Cubans and 12,400 Haitians had been absorbed by America at a cost of more than half a billion dollars.

In the 1980 presidential election, Ronald Reagan, a conservative, a former actor, and a former governor of California, decisively defeated President Carter. Candidate Reagan was a masterful and affable speaker and a reassuring public presence. But his victory was based on other factors.

Since Nixon's narrow election in 1968, the Republican Party had carefully crafted a "southern strategy" to win white votes in the southern states. Republicans denounced "forced busing" and opposed busing children to achieve school integration. The party opposed affirmative action and the use of racial quotas designed to end racial discrimination in employment. The Republicans called both quotas and affirmative action programs "reverse discrimination," claiming they took jobs from white people and gave them to people of color. As the job market shrunk, such appeals to white self-interest hit home.

Reagan was able to project these viewpoints in a jaunty, charming way. However projected, code words such as "forced busing" and "reverse discrimination" reassured white voters that this candidate and his party opposed federal help for minorities.

Reagan's managers mastered the art of sending white voters coded or hidden messages about race. The Republican candidate chose to launch his bid for the White House from Philadelphia, Mississippi. Perhaps the symbolic value of Philadelphia related simply to his party's commitment to the "southern strategy." But that town had a symbolic meaning of a different kind. Since 1964, it was associated in the public mind with the Ku Klux Klan murder of three civil rights workers, a crime that shocked the nation.

Philip Habib

Philip Habib was born in New York City in 1920 to Lebanese Maronite Christian immigrants and grew up in a largely Jewish neighborhood in nearby Brooklyn. For three decades Habib served in the U.S. Foreign Service in Asia and the Middle East. He worked with both the Democratic and Republican administrations and built a reputation as a tough and skilled negotiator.

Sometimes Habib's wisdom was ignored. He pressed President Johnson for a negotiated settlement in Vietnam, but Johnson and his advisors escalated the war. Later Habib became a leading troubleshooter for President Ronald Reagan in both Asia and the Middle East. He is credited with persuading President Ferdinand Marcos to leave the Philippines peacefully and convincing the Palestine Liberation Organization (PLO) to leave Lebanon. When no one else could, he once arranged a cease-fire in Lebanon. For that last achievement President Ronald Reagan awarded Habib a Presidential Medal of Freedom. "I might not do what he said," Henry Kissinger commented about Habib, "but I wouldn't make a move without finding out what he thought." Habib died in 1992 at 72. ■

But on that occasion, and on that spot, he failed to condemn it and did not even mention it. Reagan appeared to demonstrate that his Republican Party was the white man's party.

The Republican "southern strategy" worked in 1980. Reagan won the entire South except for Georgia, Carter's home state. Reagan's landslide swept the Democratic president from office, gathering 489 electoral votes to 49 for Carter.

The new president offered his conservative agenda as an alternative to many goals proposed by women and minorities. President Ronald Reagan vigorously promoted "family values" which he defined as prayer in public schools and making abortion illegal. Calling government "the problem," he reduced taxes for the poor by 8 percent, for the rich by 35 percent, and on corporations by 40 percent. This ultimately led to sharp cuts in funding for welfare programs, such as food stamps, Medicaid, student loans, child nutrition programs and Aid to Families with Dependent Children.

Reagan's appointments to the Supreme Court and other federal courts reflected his political views. Although he appointed Sandra Day O'Connor to the Supreme Court and continued the tradition of choosing a woman for his cabinet, he did little else for women.

At first President Reagan opposed the Voting Rights Act but finally signed the extension passed by Congress. He opposed a national holiday to honor Dr. Martin Luther King, Jr., and hinted that King might have been a Communist. But he finally agreed to sign the law and apologized to Mrs. King for his remark.

The Ku Klux Klan used Reagan's rhetoric about reverse discrimination and busing. But when an African American family's home was firebombed in Maryland, President Reagan arrived to stand with the family on their lawn and to denounce the Klan and racial violence.

Reagan picked an African American, Samuel Pierce, Jr., as his secretary of housing and urban development. But African Americans, whose gains in employment, home-buying, and education had reached a high in the 1960s, reached a low in the 1980s. By 1985, the black unemployment rate of 16.3 percent was more than two and a half times the white rate.

Blacks lost federal posts they had once held. African American members of the foreign service, 8.3 percent under Carter, fell to 6.3

percent under Reagan. The number of African American ambassadors fell from 14 under Carter to 7 under Reagan. For the first time in 24 years a president replaced the chair of the Commission on Civil Rights (CCR) with a political appointment. Reagan also replaced three other officers with people opposed to affirmative action.

The Civil Rights Division of the Department of Justice had vigorously supported enforcement of minority rights. Under Reagan, it entered cases to oppose affirmative action. The Reagan administration also reversed a policy of 11 years that denied tax exemption to private educational institutions that practiced racial discrimination. However, a public uproar convinced the president to abandon the new policy.

Julius Chambers of the NAACP Legal Defense Fund (LDF) reported,

> LDF used to be able to count on the federal government as an active partner in civil rights enforcement. Since 1981, the department is more often than not fighting us every step of the way in voting rights, school desegregation, equal employment opportunity, and affirmative action. I felt the weight of the burden of this change. Battling the federal government is both disheartening and expensive.

By 1985, the National Urban League's report, *The State of Black America*, found a nation "moving toward a state of being permanently divided between the haves and have-nots." It also noted that white America did not much care. John Jacobs concluded,

> There is also the incalculable cost of the psychic damage sustained in black America where job and income deprivation create an unhealthy atmosphere in which it is difficult to sustain the moral and social stability of individuals, the family, and the community.

Out of 83 federal appeals court appointments, President Reagan named only one African American, Lawrence Pierce. President Bush, who followed Reagan into the White House, appointed only one Black, Clarence Thomas. Reagan and Bush, in 12 years of office and with 115 appointments to the federal court of appeals, chose only two African Americans.

FURTHER READING

Barron, Milton, ed. *Minorities in a Changing World*. New York: Alfred A. Knopf, 1967.

Bernardo, Stephanie. *The Ethnic Almanac*. Garden City, NY: Doubleday, 1981.

Carson, Clayborne, et al. ed. *The Eyes on the Prize Civil Rights Reader: Documents, Speeches, and Firsthand Accounts from the Black Freedom Struggle, 1954-1990*. New York: Penguin, 1991.

Daniels, Roger. *Coming to America: A History of Immigration and Ethnicity in American Life*. New York: HarperCollins, 1990.

Debo, Angie. *A History of the Indians of the United States*, rev. ed. Norman, OK: University of Oklahoma Press, 1984.

The Ethnic Chronology Series. Dobbs Ferry, NY: Oceana Publications, 1972-1990.

Evans, Sara M. *Born for Liberty: A History of Women in America*. New York: Free Press, 1989.

Franklin, John Hope. *From Slavery to Freedom: A History of Negro Americans*, rev. ed. New York: Alfred A. Knopf, 1988.

The *In America* Series. Minneapolis, MN: Lerner Publications, 1971-1990.

Millstein, Beth and Bodin, Jeanne, eds. *We, the American Women: A Documentary History*. New York: Ozer Publishing, 1977.

Moquin, Wayne, ed. *A Documentary History of the Mexican Americans*. New York: Praeger, 1971.

Seller, Maxine S. *To Seek America: A History of Ethnic Life in the United States*. Englewood, NJ: Ozer Publishing, 1977.

_____. *Immigrant Women*. Philadelphia: Temple University Press, 1981.

Takaki, Ronald T. *Strangers from a Different Shore: A History of Asian Americans*. New York: Penguin Books, 1990.

Thernstrom, Stephan, ed. *Harvard Encyclopedia of American Ethnic Groups*. Cambridge, MA: Belknap Press, 1980.

INDEX